Public Relations for Libraries

CONTRIBUTIONS IN LIBRARIANSHIP AND INFORMATION
SCIENCE

Series Editor: Paul Wasserman

Editor

Allan Angoff

Public Relations for Libraries

Essays in Communications Techniques

Contributions in Librarianship and Information Science
Number 5

Greenwood Press
Westport, Connecticut ○ London, England

Library of Congress Cataloging in Publication Data

Angoff, Allan.
    Public relations for libraries.

    (Contributions in librarianship and information
science, no. 5)
    Includes bibliographical references.
    1. Public relations—Libraries. I. Title.
II. Series.
Z716.3.A63   659.2'9'027   72-776
ISBN 0-8371-6060-X

Library of Congress Catalog Card Number: 72-776
ISBN: 0-8371-6060-X
First published in 1973
Greenwood Press, a division of Williamhouse-Regency Inc.
51 Riverside Avenue, Westport, Connecticut 06880
Manufactured in the United States of America

Contents

Introduction

Public relations is communication. If you can communicate the essence of your library to the appropriate audience, to the people for whom it has so much to offer, if you can somehow fix the library in their minds as a resource of incalculable value, and if you can do it in a manner so effective that it brings them to the library or makes the library an important personal interest, then you have achieved the prime objective of library public relations.

Communication includes the media—newspapers, radio, television—and it also includes library bulletins listing new books and talks by staff members to local clubs and student organizations. It demands a competent and willing staff alert to the motivations of the people whose support is important in maintaining the library as a major member of the academic, urban, rural, or corporate community.

These are the elements of the public relations function. They must be utilized to the full to establish the library as the incomparable asset of any organization. The library public relations department assumes that the library offers an utterly unique service, that the library is the abiding aristocrat of our culture, and probably the most stable educational force in our society. This is a premise that can easily be defended, but far more formidable is the task of awakening the affinity for the library that most men and women possess. It can be said that the library public relations department seeks to stimulate their need by revealing in emphatic fashion the resources and varied services of the library.

It is important to stress this role of public relations and to differentiate it from the press agentry and kindred schemes that call attention to the library in theatrical fashion, but leave unprobed the true dormant interest in and receptivity to the library. A famous actress telling how she conquered alcoholism will draw 325 people to the library auditorium, but a large proportion of those people will not return to the library except to listen to another celebrity. But the patron properly alerted to the endless resources of a library in poetry, business reference books and services, travel literature, the history of ancient Rome or modern Greece, may return repeatedly, lured by books, magazines, newspapers, recordings, and a staff waiting to serve him. That patron may have been awakened to his needs; the other patron, the one who came to see a popular figure of the stage or television, attended a spectacle, with the library the incidental locale for the event.

But awakening and stimulating an audience that does not fully comprehend its own interests requires skilled practitioners, and it is here that library public relations reveals its greatest deficiency. Most libraries do not have a department or even an individual whose major or part-time responsibility is public relations. Here and there in some of the very large metropolitan libraries there are public relations departments, but in most suburban libraries, in almost all school, public, college, and special libraries, public relations is a haphazard subordinate duty of a staff member whose major interest and responsibilities are elsewhere in the library. This is surely one reason for the neglect of libraries by communities, students, political figures, university administrators, and trustees. The library is accepted, of course, but all too often as one of the less aggressive and less troublesome candidates for the urban, university, or corporate dollar.

However, public relations methods and techniques have been used in all types of libraries in recent years. In our modern competitive and budget-conscious society, libraries have been forced to seek support among groups they either ignored or took for granted in the past. Gradually they have built a large and valuable reservoir of public relations information gathered by librarians and others who have succeeded in solving serious library problems by means of good public relations. It is notable that not one of the librarians who has contributed to this volume has been trained in public relations or devotes full time to this activity. Most are library directors who have found public relations an integral part of administration at the highest executive level. Their ideas and the manner in which they have put them to work for the library should be shared by the entire library profession. The essays that follow have been selected accordingly.

Allan Angoff, *editor*

ALLAN ANGOFF is Director of Public Relations and Chief of the Reference Department, Teaneck Public Library, Teaneck, New Jersey. He also serves as Consultant on Libraries and Literature and as Chairman, Domestic and International Programs, the Parapsychology Foundation, New York. He is a graduate of Boston University and holds a master's degree in library science from Columbia. He has been associated in the past with the Boston Public Library, Montclair (N.J.) Public Library, *New York Times* Editorial Library, and the Fair Lawn (N.J.) Public Library. He is a former editor-in-chief, New York University Press, and is the author or editor of several books, including *American Writing Today: Its Independence and Vigor; The Psychic Force: Essays in Parapsychology; The World Over; Hypnotism in the United States of America;* and the biography, *Eileen Garrett and the World Beyond the Senses,* scheduled for publication in 1974. Mr. Angoff is the founder and editor of the Teaneck Public Library's three-times-a-year roundup of library news, observations and reviews, TEANECK POINTS OF REFERENCE, now in its eighth year.

Introduction ix

1

Public Relations: Its Origins and Development

Edward L. Bernays

Edward L. Bernays' career as a public relations man goes back more than half a century. He is one of the pioneers of modern public relations, and has long lectured on public relations at New York, Boston, Columbia, Tufts, and other universities. His books, classics in the field, include *Crystallizing Public Opinion, Public Relations, Your Future in Public Relations,* and *Biography of an Idea.*

THE 3R'S + 2

EARLY CHILDHOOD EDUCATION CENTER

Research

Instructional Materials Center

Reasoning

It is sound editorial judgment on the part of the editor of this book to include a discussion of public relations broader than the "how to" aspect of it. No activity can be judged only by knowing how to go through the motions of carrying it out. Every activity is part of a larger whole. We can function effectively only if we have a broader frame of reference than the action itself. We must know something about its history and causation. We must understand its guiding philosophy. It is the past that determines the present and the future. Unless we have some understanding of the past of public relations, we cannot really understand the present nor can we plan for the future. It is equally important that we know the underlying principles, the philosophy that governs public relations.

Our society is too complex for us to proceed with any important activity by experience alone or by hunch or so–called insight. We must try to understand the abstract ideas that underly an activity to be able to accomplish what we are trying to do.

A short history of public relations for the reader interested in library public relations will give him a broader perspective. A knowledge of the governing principles will help to assure the validity of his actions.

But before we approach these tasks, we must define our terms, for contrary to the belief of many, communication is a two–way and not a one–way street. It is always well to know that the writer and the reader understand each other and start with the same premises.

Public relations concerns itself with the relationship between an organization and the public on which it depends for its existence. The public relations counsel, the practitioner in the field, advises his principal on his attitudes. He ascertains the adjustments and maladjustments between the social objectives of a principal and his public. He counsels his principal on conduct and attitudes needed to achieve social objectives. He then advises his principal on how to supply the public with information and on how to persuade the public to accept his objectives. Public relations includes adjustment, information, and persuasion.

The library, as is the case with most organizations, has many publics. One public is that which supplies the funds for the library's maintenance, which may or may not include another public that reads the books. There is a public from whom the books are bought. There is the public from whom trained librarians are recruited. And there is the public of the universities that teach these recruits to become librarians. There is the public of decision and policy makers in and out of government whose actions govern libraries. And of course, there is the general public, whose opinions affect the opinions of all these other publics.

Public relations counsel, the new profession, emerged in the second decade of the twentieth century as a result of logical evolution. Many varied social forces brought about a need for a societal technician in our growing, increasingly complex society who could cope with the problems of the relationships of an organization or an individual with the public on which it was dependent.

The origins of the new discipline and the new practitioner go back to earliest history. The forces that have contributed to the emergence of the profession are:

1. the development of the concept of individual freedom and acknowledgment that the desires, rights, and privileges of the individual need to be considered

2. the rise of literacy and education, with increased participation of the public in the processes of society

3. the increase in speed of transportation and communication through technological research and invention, which has brought people more closely in contact with each other

4. the growing recognition that in an increasingly complex society there was need for a separate discipline that deals with the relations of an institution with the many groups within the public on which it is dependent

5. the development of the behavioral sciences, which have cast light on the behavior of people and have produced a storehouse of knowledge about how to deal with people, on whom all institutions are dependent.

Until the dawn of the twentieth century, most institutions,

Edward L. Bernays

profit or nonprofit, were self–contained in their attitudes and actions toward the public. Those who ran them acted in a way that they thought was best for their interest, without regard to giving the matter objective scientific study or professional consideration of public attitudes or opinion. In fact, the era in this country between 1865 and the dawn of the twentieth century has been called the "public–be–damned" period.

In the latter part of the nineteenth century the Populists, agrarians, and the trade unionists developed nationwide agitation in the United States against the so–called trusts and monopolies. They were followed by the muckrakers who battled corruption in government and abuses in big business. The New York *World* fought excesses of the insurance companies, Lincoln Steffens shed light on the shame of the cities, Ida M. Tarbell exposed the antisocial actions of the Standard Oil Company, and Upton Sinclair revealed the horrors of the packinghouse industry in *The Jungle.* New mass magazines like *McClure's* and *Everybody's* offered muckrakers the opportunity and the space to protest and reveal monopolies. The movement for reform spread to the middle classes.

Business, a main target of attack, became aware of public opinion and moved to counterattack by the use of words—by advertising and the free puffs that went with the advertising, by press bureaus of their own headed by former newspapermen, and by varied other press–agent activities. Information and publicity, instead of action, would cure whatever needed to be cured, they thought. The procedure became known as whitewashing, putting a good face on the conduct of business.

Up to this time, business, taking its cue from the secrecy of the medieval guilds, had been aloof to the press and had shunned publicity. But from 1900 to 1914 a period of informing the public was ushered in, emphasizing publicity.

The statement of Henry C. Adams, made in the December, 1902 issue of the *North American Review* is typical of the faith held in publicity:

Secrecy in the administration of a power which in any way touches the interests of the community, gives birth to the suspicion that the power is unwisely or tyrannously administered. . . . The task of publicity is to allay this suspicion and the statutory definition of publicity in any particular case must be as broad as the ground of suspicion that makes appeal to it necessary. . . . Indeed, for whatever point of view from which the trust problem is considered, publicity stands as the first step in its solution.

An early proponent of this new belief in public information for business organizations was Ivy L. Lee. He urged his clients to supply information to the public about their activities. Other pioneers in such early publicity efforts were George Michaelis, Herbert Small, and George Marvin, who set up a publicity bureau in Boston around 1900. They publicized Harvard University, the Massachusetts Institute of Technology, the Boston Elevated Street Railway, and some railroads.

Top industrialists among them, Theodore N. Vail of the American Telephone and Telegraph Company, Charles M. Schwab of Bethlehem Steel, Judge Elbert Gary of United States Steel, and Daniel Willard of the Baltimore and Ohio Railroad, accepted Lee's point of view.

The "New Freedom" of Woodrow Wilson in 1913 brought a greater recognition of the power of public opinion and publicity and helped to provide a favorable climate for the future development of the profession of public relations. But it was the activity during World War I of the United States Committee on Public Information that opened the eyes of the world to the power of the word and to the power of the public. Woodrow Wilson's slogans, "Make the World Safe for Democracy" and the "War to end all wars," projected to the people of the world by his Committee on Public Information, fired imaginations everywhere. Rightfully did historians say after the war's end that words won the war. But even more important than words was worldwide recognition that the public and public understanding were at the

Edward L. Bernays

core of the survival of institutions, whatever their nature.

A new belief in the power of public opinion was brought home to the American people. This was the beginning period of professional counsel on public relations. Public opinion had helped tumble the Czar of Russia and the Kaiser from their seats of power. Throughout the Western world, the power of the people was dramatically manifested. Technology and invention aided the spread of ideas. Radio was a new communications medium that facilitated speed of transmission to many more people.

To those interested in libraries, it should be of interest that a book, our own, titled *Crystallizing Public Opinion*, helped to establish the new profession of counsel on public relations and first outlined its scope and function. During the first world war, I served with the United States Committee on Public Information here and at the Peace Conference in Paris. When I returned to the United States in early 1919, I recognized that wartime activities like those of the Committee could be turned to peacetime pursuits. We set up an office and termed our work "publicity direction." But we soon learned that this was a misnomer. The activity was broader than that and we called it "counsel on public relations."

In 1921, we were advising the publisher Horace B. Liveright on public relations, the first time any publishing firm had used such advice. We wanted to make headway with the new field. I suggested the publication of a book on the subject. He was a daring publisher and accepted a book which we called *In the Court of Public Opinion: A Study of the New Profession of Public Relations Counsel*, and he announced it in his autumn, 1922, catalogue. The book came out the following year under a new title, *Crystallizing Public Opinion*, the first book on the subject.

The chapter headings reveal the nature of the book: "The Scope of the Public Relations Counsel"; "The Increased and Increasing Importance of the Profession"; "What Constitutes Public Opinion"; "An Outline of Methods Practicable in Modifying the Point of View of a Group."

Reviews of *Crystallizing Public Opinion* varied in their appraisal. A few were generous in praise and welcomed the new profession as an important forward step in recognition of public opinion as a potent social force. Some declared the term "public relations counsel" a dignified euphemism for the glorification of the press agent. A third group, although critical, recognized the value of the new discipline.

Since the 1920s the profession and its recognition by many social forces have developed mightily. Great changes have taken place in the attitudes and actions of all groups and institutions. They have become aware of the new public relations. They have recognized that their viability depends on adjusting both attitudes and actions to public needs and desires. They have employed public relations in order to continue their existence and ensure their growth.

Naturally, in our society progress in the use of any new discipline does not proceed at the same rate of acceptance by all groups. Some social forces have used public relations more than others; some have used it less. But today there are practically no institutions of importance that do not use it to some extent.

Certainly such a vital and important segment of society as the library must practice effective public relations, in its own interests as well as in the interests of society. Books are vital to our present and our future. This means that public libraries, university libraries, and private commercial libraries must all deal intelligently with the public in order to assure the highest level of adjustment and accommodation among them. The problems of the different kinds of library may vary. But basically the principle holds, and their problems fundamentally are the same.

Libraries since the dawn of civilization have been potent resources. In ancient Thebes the inscription over the library's entrance read "Medicine For The Soul." Ancient Alexandria proclaimed the library a "hospital for the mind." In Greek the word for book and bible is the same—"biblos." This has made the concept of a book have widespread influence beyond what may be in the book itself. Only tyrants destroy books. Hitler goes down in history for many crimes, not the least of which is book burning.

Edward L. Bernays

Books continue to be as potent today as they were in ancient times. There is current belief in some quarters today that electronic media will displace books. But wiser experts do not believe this. The computer may give you information when you press a button, but in the truest sense, electronic instruments that store information for retrieval are only extensions of bound volumes on shelves. All electronic media, including radio, television, and film, depend on the wisdom of expert programmers. And this wisdom comes in great part from the study of books.

The National Book Committee has put this succinctly: "Books are the conservers, transmitters and disseminators of our cultural and intellectual heritage. . . . People must have easy access to a wide range of books if the freedom to read is to be given validity, but thirty million of our citizens have no libraries available to them. More millions lack access to bookstores."

But the dearth of libraries is not the only problem of libraries in our society. Harold Roth, a well-known authority on libraries who is associated with the Nassau County Reference Library, has ably presented the basic problems most libraries face in our society. The libraries are concerned with:

1. effective financial support for effective operation
2. application of new techniques to library operation
3. development of effective staff
4. development of techniques for using new material of all types
5. encouragement of public understanding of the uses of libraries
6. broadening the services offered by libraries
7. development of the concept of cooperation among agencies
8. development of larger and presumably more economical units of service
9. "mining the territory," that is, reaching down to all layers of society to provide the service that is needed. To that end, therefore, the overwhelming problem still is to get people to recognize that the library does have something for them and is willing and able to perform the service they need.

The library, Mr. Roth continues, referring to publicly supported libraries, must continue to compete for its share of the community dollar that will be assigned to support community activities. "For," he writes, "I see this competition continuing. I see the development of more and more areas where information is needed, must be collected, and made available. The need is for development of a broader comprehension of the library as a central educational agency operating its own linkages through its chain of command. Cooperating at all levels with other agencies such as schools and recreation departments, to the end of providing effective public service."

Certainly Mr. Roth has covered some of the basic problems publicly supported libraries face. He has broadly highlighted one problem, which George Gallup has treated in depth and which certainly is closely related to the future of our society and its libraries, that is, the reading habits of the American public. In his report on the subject issued in May 1969, Mr. Gallup points out that the reading of books has increased in the United States. The number of adults who had read a book in the month past had increased from 23 percent to 26 percent between 1965 and 1969. Most of the increase, he found, was among the college–trained segment of the population and young adults. Mr. Gallup found that the reading of books is closely correlated with education and that as the average level of education continues to increase in the future, since more will be attending high school and higher institutions of learning, the frequency of book reading should continue to move upward. Nonetheless, the public relations problems are formidable because, as Mr. Gallup discovered in this study, except for the Bible and textbooks 58 percent of American adults have never read or finished a book.

Private, special, and university libraries do not suffer, I recognize, from the non–bookreading American public. But their problems, once they are identified, will respond, hopefully, to the same public relations approach. In a democratic society, problems that depend on public understanding can be solved if a majority of the public understands the problem and expresses

Edward L. Bernays

itself in a way that will ensure that socially sound objectives are met.

How then should a librarian approach the problem of engineering the consent of his public for the goals he has set?

The first step in the engineering of consent is to identify goals. These goals may be divided into three steps: immediate goals, those attainable in a year's time or so; intermediate goals, those attainable in several years' time; and longtime goals, those to be attained over many years. In each case these goals are to be defined in as specific terms as possible.

Does the librarian, for instance, want to increase his public? It is not enough merely to want a larger public. The public sought for must be defined as specifically as possible. The same holds true for the modification of the attitudes of the different facets of the public that come into consideration. What attitudes and whose attitudes would the librarian like to modify, and when? Very often the librarian will have only a generalized goal in his mind. That is, unfortunately, not enough to carry on an effective public relations activity. This effort to define goals may well tax the librarian's imagination and sense of reality. But it is an essential first step.

The next step is research to find out whether the goals set are realizable or whether they are unrealistic or unnecessary. As a librarian he will be able to find the best sources for public opinion research. (There are a number of very good books on the subject.) After research, the librarian will know what steps to pursue next.

Of course, if the librarian has available funds, he can go directly to one of the opinion research organizations in his community. He can engage the services of a Roper or a Gallup to find out whether the goals set are realistic within the framework of the resources he has available to meet his goals, the resources of mind power, manpower, mechanics, and money. The retention of an experienced and reputable firm of public opinion fact finders will aid in estimating whether the goals are attainable and how they may be attained, the motivations and attitudes of his public and their possible response to appeals made to them. But if he has not the financial resources to engage such a firm, he does not need to give up. He can use his research as a base and proceed within the limits of his resources to be a fact finder and researcher himself to find out whether there is a potential response on the part of his public to the meeting of the goals.

In either case, he will find out whether his goals are reachable, or whether they will need to be reoriented in the light of his research. If necessary, he can modify his goals to meet the realities of the occasion.

The next step involves the selection of the organization to carry on his public relations activity. If the library can proceed with professional aid, it can engage a professional counsel on public relations and depend on him for advice. Or if this is not feasible, the librarian can go to his shelves, check the bibliographies on public relations, and read such material as is available.

After that, the next step is, in the light of his researches and his organization, to decide on strategy. How will he use his resources of mind power, manpower, money, and materials effectively to meet the goals he has set? Will it be a blitzkrieg or a long-range campaign? How will he combine activities aimed at immediate, intermediate, and long time goals? Again, there are books available on his own shelves that should help him in his planning.

The librarian will also determine the themes he will use with his different publics. The survey will have revealed to him what these various publics respond to. (He may have to use the old approach of giving donors a modicum of immortality by naming library shelves after them.) Human beings respond to a great variety of appeals and it is essential to know what they are.

Now the librarian will be able to plan the timing of the actions he will undertake in the fulfillment of his effort to achieve his goals. Here the media may play a role in communicating to his public the facts and background of his situation. Here the group formation of our society may serve the public interest well. (Group support can engender the support of related groups.) Again his own library may serve him by providing the know–how from the books he may have on his shelves. In my

Edward L. Bernays

memoirs, *Biography of an Idea*, and in books that are listed in the several bibliographies on public relations, he will find books to guide him in his actions. The National School Public Relations Association in Washington, associated with the National Education Association, has an Edward L. Bernays Foundation Public Relations Library which has titles he may need to complete this part of his program.

The task may look complicated for the nonprofessional, but we must here recall one truism about our American system: The most potent element in it is the individual citizen. Our history is filled with examples of one–man crusades that were successful. And even in our complex society today there is evident proof of this. Rachel Carson brought us to a realization of the importance of preserving our environment; Jessica Mitford changed the patterns of the economics of dying in this country; Ralph Nader had a mighty impact on the consumer movement. And there are men of the past we all remember, such figures as Horace Mann in education, for example, who have modified patterns of attitudes and actions of the American public.

The assumption of leadership in this country is leadership, if effectively applied. Every librarian can use public relations to further his activities in the public interest, singly or with a competent professional adviser. In a highly competitive society in which every good cause is competitive with every other cause for the attention and action of the public, public relations becomes an important adjunct to the future viability of libraries.

2

Public Relations for the Metropolitan Library

Edward J. Montana, Jr.

Edward J. Montana, Jr., is Assistant to the Regional Administrator, Eastern Massachusetts Regional Library System, Boston Public Library, and Editor of the *Eastern Region News*. He is chairman of the publications committees of the Boston Public Library and the Massachusetts Library Association and a member of the publications committee of the American Library Association. He holds a bachelor's and master's degree from Boston College and a master's in library science from Simmons College.

The large urban public library has much in common with the smaller institutions, but in some ways is essentially different. Bigness is not always its own reward. Smaller public libraries are concerned with their relevance in today's society, and, in seeking to cope with this, have to decide just how far they want to go on the road to becoming centers of recreation as well as learning. Will the smaller institution try to increase its research resources so as to qualify as a reference center, or will it rely on the nearest urban library or regional headquarters for this service?

The large urban public library must resolve these same points magnified several times because they have not only strong reference sections but also large numbers of branch libraries (similar to small municipal libraries). The dilemma of research versus popular activities becomes extremely acute at this level, especially when funds are short. All of this has a public relations aspect to it, but there is the added question of the very size of the institution. It is difficult to think of these huge leviathans, sitting in their parks or squares, in human terms. They are too big for that. Both patron and staff may tend to feel that the service and the operation of the library have become impersonal and not sufficiently attentive to the needs of the individual. The staff itself becomes harried by the hordes of users on busy days and assistance becomes mechanical and perfunctory. This leaves the patron unsatisfied and frustrated. The Administration, for its part, worrying over rising costs, lack of space, or expansion plans, may forget some of the niceties of smooth operation, and, in the interests of getting results, alienates the very people it is trying to help. Anyone who has walked into a large urban library and seen a sign reading RENEWAL OF BOOKS AND PERIOD-ICALS IS NOT ALLOWED at one of the first points of contact might compliment the institution on its directness, but certainly not on its tact, to say nothing of its courtesy toward the people who use it.

The large public library is different, too, because it serves a wider variety of publics, including substantial minority groups, and people in all categories of age, income, and education. The reputation of the urban library is apt to be based, to a large extent, on its research collections, which is only to be expected. They are the institutions with the resources and the staff to serve as centers for the accumulation and dispensation of knowledge. The cultural reputation of a nation is based on organizations such as these. But although their value for research is essential, and although everything possible must be done to maintain this capacity, it should also be remembered that, because of this, the urban library has two faces, and one is as important as the other. Research facilities, despite their incalculable value, are used by comparatively few people, as against the total population. And the more special the collections, the more valuable they are, but they are also less used, again relatively speaking.

Thus a public library that concentrates on its research collections to the detriment of its services to the general public will be, sooner or later, in a precarious position. This is all the more true when a system serves as a headquarters' library for a given geographic unit. When this is the case, the urban library will find itself being used, more and more, by patrons from the areas in its region but outside its city limits. The libraries in the region will be only too glad to have the headquarters bear the cost of good reference service, but will nevertheless be very unhappy if it does not provide them with additional materials with which to serve their own publics. These may be books, films, records, advertising materials, centralized technical services, or anything else that will make their institutions more immediately vital and relevant to their communities.

Service, of course, is *the* word. Without it, all of the public relations in the world is not going to help.

Service begins with materials and their accessibility, and runs the whole gamut of the process of getting the right book (or film, or manuscript, or recording) to the right person at the right time. How this is done is part of the regular administrative procedure. Making sure the patrons know what is being done and why and how these procedures can operate to their benefit is the job of the public relations director.

Public relations is primarily concerned with letting people

Edward J. Montana, Jr.

know what is going on: that the library is there for their profit, what it has to offer, and how it can be used on all levels. Library promotion can be included here also, i.e., not only a simple factual presentation, but an urging of the public on the part of the library to make use of its services for their own betterment. (It cannot be taken for granted that merely because a product is good, the public will rush to use it; this is not always true. Assuming that everyone knows about it, most will still have to be convinced that they *ought* to use it.)

Keeping the library in the public's mind continually by fostering community relations and a steady buildup of goodwill among the various elements of a community by telling the "library's story," to use a hackneyed phrase, will do much to ensure not only its widespread use but also widespread support when it is needed.

In setting up a formal public relations program, the personality and working habits of the personnel, especially at the top level, are of prime importance. Rushing to meet a deadline at short notice can be a harrowing experience and is not for the lover of peace and quiet. Many of the qualities required will be the same as for other library staff members: ability to get along with people, sincerity, and stick–to–itiveness. In addition, a public relations person must be able to write easily, clearly, quickly, and well; must have had—and have—sufficient social experience so that he will know a story that will catch the public's interest when he sees one, and be able to interpret it in terms that will appeal to the reader (or listener or viewer, if the medium is radio or television). He should have a college degree, preferably in one of the liberal arts, wide interests, a critical eye, and a ready acceptance of new ideas and ways. Previous experience in the fields of journalism, advertising, publishing, or the social services is also valuable.

Whether or not a PR director needs a library science degree is often debated. Theoretically, a person who has been through library school will understand the workings of the system better than the one who has not. On the other hand, he may understand them too well. In a very real sense, the PR worker is the public's representative on the library's staff. He must see everything from two points of view: that of the patron and that of the library administration, and be able to interpret one to the other.

The PR officer should have an assistant—someone who can carry on when he is away—at least one artist; a varityper operator (or immediate and direct access to one); and a secretary. The assistant may have the same general characteristics and background, but little or no previous experience. His position could be in the nature of an apprentice. The artist should be a graduate of an accredited art school. One who has majored in fine arts with some courses in commercial art may be acceptable, but a commercial arts major is to be preferred. The artist should present a portfolio of *original* art work illustrating the various aspects of his artistic talent and creative ability when he is being interviewed for employment. Versatility is of prime importance. He should also have had enough experience with various presses so that he will know their capabilities, and exactly how his art work will look after it is printed.

The current practice is for printing sections to be part of the business operations of the library setup and so do not have to be discussed here except to say that the public relations officer should maintain close contact with this department and be aware of its workings and potential.

Whether there is a separate exhibits office depends on how deeply the library wants to commit itself in this area and how much space it has to fill. The general attitude is that when exhibits are being considered, another member or two is added to the public relations office, rather than setting up an additional administrative unit.

External public relations are those that involve people outside of the library. These are the people—including legislators, potential donors, civic leaders, and the general public— who must, first, be informed of what the library can offer them, and who, secondly, may let the library know their needs, so that it can, if possible, fill them.

The services of the library may be divided into the general

Edward J. Montana, Jr.

and the specific. The general are those ongoing services that are available all the time, whereas the specific includes special programs, one time events or series of events, and so forth. Newspapers, radio and television, newsletters, and other publications are all means of informing the public and can serve for both types of services.

The chosen method of informing the newspapers of library services or events is the newspaper release. The following are suggestions for writing a release drawn up by Mrs. Barbara Michaels, Director of Public Relations and Exhibits at the Newton (Mass.) Free Library. Newton is a residential city of approximately 100,000, and so does not really qualify as one of the larger urban areas. However, the instructions are excellent, and will be useful to anyone.

How to Crank up your Library Publicycle and Get it Rolling

If you drew a picture of the shape of of a news release, it would be an inverted triangle, Like this:

first sentence

You spill the beans in the first sentence, and then keep dribbling throughout the story.

paragraph structure

Each paragraph should diminish in importance to the whole story, so if the editor doesn't have enough space for what you have written, he can cut your release (also called a handout) off at a paragraph's end, and still have an entity.

first paragraph	The first paragraph, or *lead*, should entice the reader into the story and make him want to read on.
what comes first isn't necessarily first	SO FORGET EXPOSITORY STYLE. FORGET CHRONOLOGY. Ask yourself: what is the outstanding thing about this story? And write about that first.
rule of c	BE COLORFUL, CORRECT, CONCRETE, COMPLETE, AND EVEN A BIT KOOKY.
rule of w	Remember all those w's (who, what, when, where, why). But also remember the c's.
role of pizzaz	Bring into play some pizzaz—in the form of a provocative question; or alliteration; or an interesting parallel or difference; or concrete figures. Look in the dictionary and learn proofreader's marks.
release heading	When you write your release, and send either a clear mimeo copy or an original to each place, the heading should look like this:

Newton Free Library   April 22, 1970
414 Centre Street
Newton, Mass. 02158   527-7700

Virginia A. Tashjian
City Librarian   *For Release May 28, 1970*
                                    (or)
                          (FOR IMMEDIATE RELEASE)

22   Edward J. Montana, Jr.

organization of release for typist	And then start your story. It should be double (or triple) spaced, with wide margins everywhere. Don't bother with carbons except for your own records. Newspapers hate 'em. Use a good stiff paper with no show through.
numbering	Number your pages. Don't split paragraphs at the bottom of the page. This makes problems for the printer.
hyphens	Don't hyphenate at the end of a line; it's confusing to the printer.
more than one page	At the bottom of the first page, do this:

–more–

at the end	At the end of the story, do this:

–end–

length of story	If you can't tell your story in 3 pages, forget it. No newspaper will look at a library story which is over 3 pages (also called *takes*).
numerals	For newspaper purposes, always write numbers in numerals. UNLESS the number starts the sentence (i.e., Ten talented troupers . . . .).
	Send your releases to your local radio station.
be correct	use everybody's name and give proper titles, credits.

other places than newspapers	Remember usefulness of college alumni bulletins, trade papers, house organs.
headlines	LET THE EDITOR PUT ON THE HEADLINE. T'aint polite to do it yourself.
more than one paper in town	If you have more than one paper in your town (dailies and weeklies), and send the same exact story to each, don't expect a byline. If you send different copy to each, the editor may give you a byline.
deadlines	Respect deadlines. Ayer's Directory will give you this information.
photos	IF YOU INCLUDE PHOTO-GRAPHS, and you should, when you can:
how many in a photo	*Be ruthless.* No more than two people to a picture. It's unprofessional to have one of those people be *you.*
what to do	Don't let them look directly into the camera. Have the people do something—fiddle with a camera, adjust an easel, hold a paintbrush. SOMETHING.
photo i.d.	Type out identification, and fold over end of picture, attaching with bit of scotch tape.
photo return	Don't ask your editor to return the photo. It's a pain in the neck.

Edward J. Montana, Jr.

word of wisdom	Do your homework, be accurate, respect deadlines, and your library will make the news every time.
Ayer's Directory	Use your Ayer's Directory. It's a pal.
how to wheel a story	As you become enthusiastic about writing releases, you should begin to *wheel* your story, using the same facts to write stories for different places.
different lead paragraphs	For instance, if a Melrose native works in Concord and is going to give a slide–talk in Newton (these are cities in the Metropolitan Boston area), there are three separate lead paragraphs you should write. And if he is a University of Massachusetts graduate with a Master's from University of Georgia, there are two more shots, if you have the time.
	In each case, alter the lead paragraph so as to give the local angle its proper prominence.
editors	Know your editors—gardening, photography, etc. Just call the paper and ask the switchboard operator. Keep your list up to date.
lists of books?	Do include title, author, publisher of a book or two in your stories, OCCASIONALLY. But don't expect your paper to publish long lists of book titles. Nobody cares.
people like people	DO HANG YOUR STORIES on personalities. Personnel in the library.

Their specialities, collections, courses, conferences, honors, for local newspapers. Metropolitan papers will also be especially interested in the trustees, director, important visitors or speakers when their activities are of citywide or regional importance. People are interested in people. And bring in your library via the soft sell.

When you write a release make sure that you really have something to say, and something that the newspaper's readers will be interested in knowing. It is not a good idea to let the editors get in the habit of seeing the letterhead, say "it's from the library" and push it to one side.

Radio and television must also be used. Radio and TV stations are required to devote a certain amount of time to public service advertising, but are under no obligation to grant time to any *specific* group. In addition, many stations, in the name of goodwill, will go beyond the specified time if they think the subject is worthwhile.

Station time can be used for spot announcements, to advertise library services in general, or one, or a group of programs; a regular series of programs, usually once a month and lasting for fifteen minutes or half an hour, during which some aspect of the library's ongoing services or programs are described and discussed; news items on regular local broadcasts regarding some special event or announcement the library wishes to make; or the interview type of show where a representative of the library answers questions of public interest put to him by the show's leading personality.

Television spot announcements require some visual accompaniment, most effectively in color. The library can use photographs of its own from which the station or a commercial firm can make slides at moderate expense. For something more elaborate it is probably best to buy a series that has been produced

Edward J. Montana, Jr.

by an agency for general distribution. For each library to make its own is not only unnecessary but also extremely expensive. Two series of high quality already in existence are those originating from the libraries of New York State and the Pennsylvania State Library. The first is in animated cartoon style with a musical background and is general in nature; the second uses live action photography and describes library services a little more specifically. Both series are used in parts of the country other than those in which they originated and have proven their usefulness.

When there is an important library presentation on the stations, make sure that it is adequately publicized, in the library and staff newsletters, at least. (This is assuming that the station warns you far enough in advance, which is not always the case.)

Some specific do's and don'ts are as follows:

DO . . . Submit all program copy to the program director as far in advance as possible. Ten days would not be too soon.

DO . . . Get news releases to the news director as early as you can—a week in advance, if possible.

DO . . . Typewrite all copy *triple space* on 8½ × 11 inch paper, using one side only. Start one–third down the first page. Leave ample margins.

DO . . . Use a clean ribbon for *legible* copy. Provide extra copies as requested.

DO . . . Put the name of your organization, and your own name, address, and telephone number at the top of each item.

DO . . . Give all the facts—the what, when, where, who, and why of your event. Be sure to give specific starting and ending dates, such as "Use between July 4 and July 7," not "Monday through Thursday."

DO . . . Write all copy for the voice—a bit more informal in style than copy written only for the eye. If you normally use "don't" in oral conversation, write it that way in your script. Use "let's" instead of "let us."

A good rule: Be informal, but don't be breezy.

DO . . . Provide a biographical sketch of any person to be interviewed, along with six or eight points to be covered. If the name is difficult to pronounce, give the phonetic spelling.

For Radio

DO . . . Time spot announcements to run 10 seconds (25 words), 20 seconds (50 words) or 60 seconds (150 words).

DO . . . Use simple, descriptive words that form pictures, give dimension and color. Radio reaches only the ear and the listener must be able to sketch in his own mind the picture you are trying to create.

DO . . . Submit several copies of all material—and make sure the last one is as legible as the first.

For Television

DO . . . Check with the program or news director on slides, films, and photographs that can be used to "demonstrate" your message.

DO . . . Make sure copy written to accompany such visual aids "fits" with the slide, film, or photo shown.

DO . . . Time your copy at a slightly slower pace than for radio. Standard announcements for television run 10 seconds (about 20 words), 20 seconds (40 words) and 60 seconds (125 words).

DO . . . Provide one slide or photograph for each 10–second spot; two for a 20–second spot, etc.

DO . . . Keep in mind that slides are preferable in most cases to photographs. They can be made professionally at minimum cost. When photographs are used, matte or dull–surfaced prints are preferable, since glossy prints reflect studio lights.

DO . . . Request return of your visual material if you want to preserve it. Otherwise, it may be thrown away.

Edward J. Montana, Jr.

DON'T . . . Ask for public service time to publicize or promote bingo parties or lotteries.

DON'T . . . Try to use free air time to extol the advantage of any commercial product.

DON'T . . . Plead, beg, or threaten in an attempt to get time. A good presentation in the public interest will stand on its own merits.

DON'T . . . Submit copy scribbled on scratch paper or on a postcard. Writing in longhand invites errors.

DON'T . . . Omit essential information. Check over your copy to be sure it tells the who, what, why, when, and where, and includes your name, address, and phone number.

DON'T . . . Get carried away by trivialities, superlatives, and over-enthusiasm. Omit adjectives and avoid nicknames.

DON't . . . Abbreviate telephone numbers. "FE" might be FEDERAL or it might be FENTWORTH. Never abbreviate or hyphenate any words in a script.

DON'T . . . Use onionskin paper for on–the–air copy. It rattles![1]

Whether the public relations director is dealing with newspapers, radio, or television, before any information campaign is begun, he should make himself known to the people who will be using his material. In large cities there will often be someone—such as a director of public or community services or an executive editor—who can be contacted. An appointment should be arranged, and the newspaper or station's policies discussed. The library's representative should explain just what he is trying to do and then follow the advice of the editor (of whatever media). These people are one of the keys to the library's information program and should not be regarded as "enemies" or competitors. Neither should it be forgotten that the media are in business, a business that, in the last analysis, must show a profit (in the monetary sense) or cease to exist. The editor may be sympathetic to your aims but he is not going to do much for you unless what you have in mind is going to appeal to his readers or viewers. Many National Library Week editorials, for example, have gone down the drain, year after year, simply because of the language in which they were written, only to be finally accepted when the writer tied the subject onto some widely known and widely recognized event or current expression of speech. This was true even though the information in the editorial was roughly the same in each instance. It was simply making the library's message relevant.

Publications are a basic source for spreading the library's message, and they fall into three general categories.

The first involves the more weighty releases: the studies. Hard or soft bound, they are issued as contributions to the world's knowledge. Based on the specialized collections of the library, they are usually, but not always, associated with rare book departments or large special collections, but they may be issued by any area that has primary source materials within its jurisdiction. Catalogs of these sources may also be printed, as may lists of new acquisitions, although the latter really belong in the third category noted below.

The distribution of these publications varies, depending on the method of issuance. If the library itself does the printing then it usually handles the whole job; if a commercial publisher, then it will be processed just as is any other trade book, although the library may keep sufficient copies on hand so that it may act as one (and possibly the principal) of the vendors.

Whatever the method, the library will want to see that the book has as much publicity as possible. Copies should be sent to the reviewers of the pertinent journals and leaders in the field. If the work concerns art or music, for example, a public function, by invitation, might be held to introduce the book, adding a tour of the department involved with a general explanation of its strengths. The press should be asked and so should any individuals with an interest in the field who might be willing to sponsor publication of another title, based, ideally, on a group of items that he will contribute to the library or allow the library to purchase through his patronage.

It goes without saying that, regardless of how crucial the subject matter, the work should be properly designed with as many illustrations as possible, and with some in color, although the

Edward J. Montana, Jr.

latter may be impractical because of the cost. Drabness is no longer the "in" thing in the publishing world, and the old maxim that the duller the format the more valuable the content no longer holds.

Works of this type should be published by a public library. They are an effective way of bringing the library's resources before a wider audience and of enhancing the institution's reputation in the field of scholarship. The influence of these publications is enormous even though their scope may be narrow.

The second type cannot be called scholarly in the restricted sense, although it does add to the fund of knowledge, or, better stated, is an aid in that direction. These are bibliographies of more or less permanent interest, of wide scope, and limited to one subject field or an allied group of subjects. It may be a lengthy list of works published within a given period on a given subject, recommended titles on a particular theme (current topics such as the environment, the city, juvenile guidance, are a fertile field for this type of work). The point is that it has more than casual use and will be valuable for a long period of time. Because of the cost, they may have to be sold—at least to interested parties outside of the library's immediate area—but for as modest a price as practical.

These publications will have a greater distribution than those in class one, as they will have wider use for schools, civic groups, and neighborhood leaders as well as parts of the general public. If the topic is of civic interest, pollution, for example, sample copies should be sent to those most closely involved: political, social, and civic leaders; conservation groups; and prominent private citizens interested in the topic. Depending on the person to whom the copy is being given, a brief message could be enclosed expressing the library's compliments and noting that additional copies can be obtained, with their cost. This information might be on a specially designed card or sheet, and the price (including postage), the address to which the check should be sent, and to whom the check should be made out should all be clearly stated. The address ought to include not only the street, city, and zip code, but also a specific department and/or person to whom the check is to be sent. If orders are accepted without payment and a bill sent, these same instructions should also be included; otherwise checks will arrive addressed only to the library and with no hint as to what is being paid for.

The above is especially pertinent when a library does not have a separate sales office and the procedures are being handled by the issuing department or the public relations personnel. When there is a separate sales office, regular business procedures will apply.

The third main category is made up of the so–called "give-aways." These are the reading lists, including bookmarks and triple folds, for all age groups and on all subjects that are distributed free of charge by the public library. They contain suggestions for reading in various fields and in connection with a multitude of events from Jewish Book Month to Christmas. Of no great intellectual pretensions, these publications are still, in a sense, the most important that a library can issue. They are one of the best ways the library has of reaching the community. Comparatively inexpensive to reproduce, they can be printed in large quantities and widely distributed. Available at the charge-out desk, they lead the reader through a maze of titles to several on a particular topic that interests him. Needless to say, the library should have the books available that are suggested on the list.

The value of these materials will be somewhat wasted, however, if the library is the only place where they can be found. If the list is on gardens, the garden clubs should get supplies; if on drugs, the churches, youth centers, and counseling services, as well as the junior and senior high schools. If a librarian goes anywhere to give a book talk, a supply of lists should go with him, and they may also be distributed at programs related to the subject covered.

Posters fall into this category, too. The type that will get the most use is a general one, simply urging the viewer to visit his public library, or advertising a type of service, e.g., large print books. Others, of a narrower nature, can call attention to a program or series of programs.

Edward J. Montana, Jr.

If well designed, in the commercial sense, a poster will be readily accepted and displayed by commercial firms, banks, labor unions, and other groups. If part of a chain, these organizations will have central offices, usually with a director of public relations. Once the material is accepted (and most will not commit themselves until after they have seen it), the required number can be shipped to them and they will take care of the distribution. Otherwise, the time–honored method of going from place to place will have to be used.

Departmental guides are useful items to have. They briefly describe the department involved, mention special collections, hours—especially if they are different from the library as a whole—special services, and lending policy, in detail if necessary.

A general events calendar should be available for the central library and its subsidiary units. The best type is an annual, separating different kinds of programs and arranging them month by month. If the program schedule is heavy, there could be separate publications for the main unit and the branches, with those of several branches in the same area being combined. Monthly calendars are also useful, but they have the disadvantage of having to be prepared and issued ten or twelve times per year, and once in the patron's hands give him comparatively little time to plan his own schedule.

A newsletter is a necessary companion to the calendar. It does not need to be published as often, and should not be, unless there is something of interest to be written about. It can pick out special events also listed on the calendar but unless these are of city— or area wide—importance, this is a profitless venture, and a waste of space.

The newsletter is the voice of the library, and many library-oriented items that will not be covered by the press or news programs, or covered only in part, can be featured here. For example, if a new building is planned, to choose the most spectacular item, it will probably be announced in the news media, briefly; when it is completed there will be pictures (very few if it is a branch library), and a brief description. The newsletter

The Metropolitan Library   33 can go into the details, noting the cost, special architectural features, and, especially, new or expanded services to the patrons. Personnel can also be introduced—briefly—and an invitation to visit and borrow extended. Speakers of national renown can also be described, continuing series of programs, new services, changes in library policy, and so on.

The newsletter should be non-technical—library jargon should be avoided here as elsewhere—well–illustrated, and informative. The public will want to know, above all, how the events, changes, and so forth, are going to affect them (and if they are going to be affected, this is one of the places where they should be told), and not how it is going to affect the library internally. They don't care. Staff news should, on the whole, be omitted, and so should the technical side of running a library, unless there is going to be some *direct* effect on the user.

The newsletter may be distributed at the information desk and other key points throughout the main library, at the charge desks of the branches, and through a regular mailing list. The mailing list may include members of the public who live in the city or in the metropolitan area, but because of distance, illness, or other reason cannot visit the main library or one of the branches; civic leaders and elected officials; members of the cultural community; and, if the library is a regional headquarters, the member libraries. Reciprocal arrangements for quantity distribution can sometimes be made with other agencies in the city, e.g., museums. Private businesses with large staffs located near the library will also often want large numbers of copies to post and distribute among their employees.

Flyers are the most ephemeral publications of all. They are issued about two weeks prior to the event, and after it is over are as timely as yesterday's newspaper. And yet care should be taken in their preparation. The flyer is used not only to advertise the program but also to encourage the viewer to attend. And while no flyer will compensate for a dull program, a program is not successful if no one goes. Mimeographing, then, should be avoided; even the most careful job looks tacky and old–fashioned. Whether varityping or printing should be used depends on the amount of time available and the importance of the program. It does not make sense to spend time on flyers that could be spent on more useful publications. An electric or selectric typewriter is often the answer. The type is clear, sharp, and attractive, and it photographs easily. The plates can then be run off on a printing machine. Simple artwork drawn right on the typed sheet is acceptable as long as there is sufficient contrast and strength of tone. A piece of artwork done separately by the staff artist, and used every month (or so) for a series of programs, e.g., those held for youth groups or senior citizens and regularly scheduled, can be pasted on the typed sheet, photographed, returned, and used again.

A few words about artwork. Selling sugar is not quite the same as selling library service, but there are many similarities behind it. The product must be presented in an attractive way, and the audience must be persuaded to use it. The library begins with an advantage: there is no satisfactory alternative once the need for it is recognized. That a vast majority of the population feels no such need is amply proved by statistics from many sources.[2] Once upon a time, people were quite satisfied to have such a cultural symbol in their midst and to support it—75% as late as 1965.[3] But this situation is changing as library costs (and those of everything else) rise; as the population increases and added costly facilities are needed; as schools, museums, and transportation systems consume more public revenue (as a matter of fact, museums are as badly off as libraries, although they have large private resources they can call on; as a result they are working, and working hard, at changing their image and emphasizing service to the many rather than the few, as if their lives depended on their success—as, indeed, it does); and as salaries rise. The result is that the public is not very willing to support something they consider merely as a symbol of prestige as much as they once were, and hours are shortened, branches are closed, and new buildings are rejected as too expensive (and unnecessary).

Librarians, then, can no longer quibble about "commercialism" or mutter about being the last preservers of culture. They have to get in there and fight for the public's attention like everyone else. There is no reason why they have to lose their dignity in the process, but after all, can libraries afford to be more conservative than banks?

Artwork then should be colorful, current, and lively. It should follow the same standards as commercials, which have advanced to the point where some television commercials are much more attractive than the programs they appear on. The American public is used to being cajoled from all sides. And it is a truism that the worth of a product means nothing until the public 1) knows about it; 2) is persuaded to use it; and 3) is satisfied with it.

Library materials, then, should be designed to compete. This is especially true of items that are going to be posted in a public area outside of the library, where they may be placed next to materials from other organizations. The ability of the viewer to turn himself off almost automatically when confronted with a piece of advertising has become phenomenal and only underlines the need for good graphics, good slogans, and something different.

When designing a poster on a specific topic, the slogan or text is more or less determined by the subject, but for one advertising libraries or library services in general, the field is wide open. The general rule of thumb is that if the slogan is mundane the artwork has to be particularly striking to be effective. A slogan should be current, e.g., "Your public library tells it like it is," or "Your public library puts it all together," so it will appeal to teenagers, but not so avant garde that the older person will not know what it means. It must have been around long enough to be recognized but not so long as to be outmoded. On the other hand, the perfectly ordinary "When was the last time you visited your public library?" can be placed under a seemingly unrelated photograph of, say, about 1900, and run on a brightly colored stock, so that the eye is caught by the design and then led to the message.

The administration of the graphics program of any library, but especially a large public library because of the potential

Edward J. Montana, Jr.

number of people involved, can mean the difference between success and failure. Some libraries use the committee system: a reading list, bookmark, program of events, e.g., for a summer reading club, is prepared by a committee and sent to the public relations officer to be designed in final form. The artist prepares a design or designs, shows them to the PR officer who submits them to the committee for discussion. The design is then returned with comments to the artist via the PR officer, the changes are made, and it is resubmitted.

Aside from the fact that this process can be interminable, the result is usually unsuccessful. Serviceable, but unsuccessful from the point of view of good graphics.

A second way might be as follows: the list is submitted to the public relations officer who turns it over to the artist with any pertinent suggestions. The design(s) is shown to and approved by the officer. It is then taken to the person immediately responsible for the list—the chairman of the committee or the adults supervisor.

The only question the latter must answer is whether or not the artwork fits the theme of the list, and if it does there is no further comment. For example, if the list concerned horses, and the PR officer, in a moment of delusion, approved a design featuring cats, the originator of the list could object. Otherwise not. Colors, design, and format are decided in the public relations office.

Several large urban libraries which have used the first approach for years (not to say decades) have tried the second way, with dramatic results. The philosophy behind the change involves the feeling that public relations officers and trained artists are just as professional and as qualified in their own fields as the subject or age specialists. Trying to work with a committee is, in any case, one of the world's most frustrating experiences, and when it involves a cultural status symbol such as art appreciation, virtually impossible. With a committee of seven, there is more than an even chance that there will be seven different opinions. People who would not dream of pontificating on science, or history, or cataloging because it is not their field will always have something to say about art. They would feel culturally deficient if they did not, and consequently are apt to be uncommonly stubborn in their opinions. The result: a watered down version of what started out as a perfectly good idea.

This does not discredit the subject specialist in any way. But each to his own. It makes as much sense for an adult committee, for example, to tell an artist how to design the cover or format of a list as it does for the artist to tell the committee what books to put on it.

Public relations should begin to operate as soon as the patron steps inside the front door. Many patrons entering a large public library for the first time, or even after many visits, are apt to be bewildered at best and, at worst—especially in the case of older people or the younger teenagers—overwhelmed and defeated. Patrons have progressed beyond the old fear of "bothering the librarian" and thus leaving without having done what they came to do because they were afraid to ask questions. But there are still some hurdles to be overcome.

A public information desk is a necessity for questions that can be answered quickly, especially of the "where do I find . . . .?" type. Since, on a busy day, business is apt to be very heavy at this point of contact, printed guides to the library could also be on hand. These would contain floor plans; general information for requesting materials and borrowing them for home use (the classes of materials that cannot be borrowed should be clearly stated); an explanation of the use of the card catalog, what it contains, the location of information on materials that it does not contain, and where the reader can get help if he has trouble finding something; library hours; regulations; and an explanation of any unusual circumstances (such as the fact that material issued before a given date is housed outside the building and will take a certain amount of time to recall).

Floor plans blown up and placed on the wall in a prominent position are also useful. One type, which is electrically lit from behind, uses the "You are here" approach with a special figure denoting the position of the person looking at the sign. The

Edward J. Montana, Jr.

viewer can then guide himself from this point to the area that he is looking for. A series of such floor plans might be hung in the main entrance lobby, and others on each floor, perhaps pertaining to that floor only. Another type is the floor plan with an automatic subject finder. The plan of the library is illuminated and each area is clearly marked. Below is a broad series of subject headings, e.g., costume, history, psychology, with a button beside each. The patron presses the button beside the subject in which he is interested and a light shines in a delimited area of the floor plans showing the department in which the material is located.

To avoid confusion, only public areas should be described on the floor plans. Those wanting to go elsewhere could inquire at the information desk.

Other signs throughout the building may note the names of departments and special collections. "How to find . . ." notices within individual departments, the classification of subject headings of the materials in a given open stack area, the location of bibliographic tools such as the *Reader's Guide*, and various general notices, from "Please excuse the inconvenience, this department is expanding" or ". . . being moved to larger quarters" to "Please return your books on time—others are waiting," should also be prominently posted.

All of these signs should be printed in clear concise language that the patron can understand. Signs using library jargon do not serve their purpose and can even reinforce the patron's feeling that he would rather be somewhere else. They also waste the staff's time, making them give the information that should have been on the signs in the first place. "Kardex," "Xerox," "vertical file," "subject entry," even "reference" and "interlibrary loan"! The librarian might as well be talking Greek. "Magazines, newspapers, and pamphlets" is clearer than "periodicals," and since the library is promoting its informational services, why not use that word instead of "reference"?

The library must have rules and regulations, but these need not be expressed in negative terms. It is a byword of good communications that "don't" and "no" as in "no renewals," or "these books may not be withdrawn," should be avoided. How much better is "these books are kept in the library so that they may be available for use at all times."

There is also no reason, except tradition, why this information has to be in heavy black type on a white card. Color can be used as well as a soft-sell and humorous approach. Cartoon-type figures and a cheerful tone can be very effective when a library policy needs to be explained that the public does not understand and about which it must be informed.

As far as the staff's attitude is concerned no more need be said than that they should know when to help and when to leave a patron alone and that a smile and a willing manner can do more to improve a library's image than almost anything else.

Programs have long been an effective means of bringing the patron into the library, and there are many different kinds for all ages. These are so familiar that they do not have to be mentioned here. But there is a new type that is being used more often and that is proving especially effective because it involves a large degree of community participation.

One of the first and most successful is the now famous "Bessie's Bash" held several years ago at the Bushwick Branch of the Brooklyn Public Library. Its official title was "Library Festival" but it gained its more popular designation because its planner and major domo was Brooklyn's Senior Community Coordinator, Miss Bessie Bullock.

The purpose of the festival was to bring about a closer relationship between the residents of the area and the library (which is housed in a rather imposing and forbidding looking building). The "bash" was held during a two–day period in June with almost continuous events scheduled from 10 A.M. to 8 P.M. the first day and from 10 A.M. to 6 P.M. the second day. There were outdoor as well as indoor activities so that everyone in the neighborhood would know what was going on.

There was a kitemaking demonstration, wood block print-ing, a lady glassblower, and a steel band concert; a production of "Hansel and Gretel," and a karate demonstration. Film programs and storytelling sessions ran continuously, and books were displayed in such unusual "racks" as a hammock and a wicker picnic basket. Talks on Negro history followed a salad-making demonstration, and individuals with creative talents provided instruction in crocheting, dressmaking, cake making, and millinery. Several Puerto Rican women brought cakes for the cake demonstration. To further involve the community, a Prince and Princess were chosen from the juvenile residents of Bushwick to reign over the festival. And topping it all off (no pun intended) huge red balloons flew from the building's roof and bore the words "Make It A Library Summer." This message was also on a banner stretched across the front of the library.

The cost of the project was mostly in staff time and effort, but little in the way of cash expenditures. A printed schedule of events, colorful posters, the balloons, 5,000 announcements, and the banner (which was reused later) all had to be paid for, but almost nothing else.

The estimate of visitors ranged from 6,000 to 8,000, and as a result the library and its staff became more human to the area's residents. A librarian who has read a boy's palm will seem much more approachable to him in the future! (My thanks to Miss Irene Moran, Director of Public Relations, Brooklyn Public Library, for the foregoing information.)

Similar programs have been staged in Los Angeles and Cincinnati, and were also very effective.[4] Commercial? Yes. But the libraries concerned are now more a part of their communities than they were before. And that is what it is all about.

Internal public relations, i.e., between the Administrative officers and the staff is, in its own way, just as important as external. Staff members should be kept informed about changes in library policy, changes in staff functions, and, in general, anything that is going to affect them. If changes are going to be made, or have been made and clarification is needed, the information should be available as quickly as possible. Keeping something completely quiet in a large system is virtually impossible, and if the Administration does not supply the answers, the rumor mills will.

Staff meetings should be held when there is something to meet about. These need not involve the entire staff, but only those above a certain level, e.g., department or section head. These people should be kept informed of matters affecting the library as a whole and their areas in particular. Every effort should be made to see that the pertinent information is reported back, by the section or department heads, to their respective staffs.

Between meetings notices of immediate importance may be circulated among the various departments and branch libraries. Each notice should be posted and initialed by every staff member so that each department head will know that all of his employees have seen it. This avoids the pleading of ignorance later.

A staff newsletter, emanating from the administrative offices (this would include the director of public relations), is also useful. It should be issued as often as there is something to report. It should be an informative sheet with items on the activities of the different members of the staff, new gifts or book collections, the rearranging of departments, and departmental services. If something of system–wide importance is to be included, everything possible should be done to make sure that the issue is distributed and read *before* the same item appears in the newspapers (which, in any case, may well be inaccurate, or include only a part of the total picture). This is essential for good morale.

The staff should also be kept up to date on the public relations program itself. A publicity manual is always handy. It explains who is responsible for what, e.g., branch librarians usually take care of the publicity on items of interest to their immediate areas, while the PR officer handles subjects of city wide interest. It contains suggestions for writing news releases; the ordering of signs, posters, flyers, and other publicity materials from the public relations office; and, in general, the procedures to be followed in keeping open the line of communication between the area library and its community.

It might also be advisable for the PR officer to attend meetings of branch librarians, and department or section heads occasionally to explain in detail any difficult procedures or to answer questions on the different aspects of the PR program.

Large urban public libraries may also be the headquarters for regional library systems. The services provided may include borrowing privileges, interlibrary loan, and reference.

It should be mentioned here that regional systems throughout the United States vary widely in size and number of member libraries. For example, the Public Library of Cincinnati and Hamilton County serves thirty–five libraries and a population of 625,000; Rochester Public Library, which is the regional headquarters for Monroe County, takes care of seventy–five members and some 586,000 people; whereas the Los Angeles County Public Library with ninety–two members and a population of 2,500,000, may be compared with the Boston Public Library, the regional headquarters of the Eastern Massachusetts Regional Library System with 210 member libraries and a population of 3,784,000.

A newsletter sent to member libraries and trustees is one of the essential ingredients of the public relations program of a regional system. The type may vary depending on the size of the system, but the basic purpose is to provide information on regional services, workshops, personnel changes at headquarters, and so on that will affect the member libraries. This may be the extent of the information given, with perhaps a few paragraphs added on the activities of the area, state, and national professional organizations, details of events such as National Library Week, and so forth.

In a large system with member libraries of different sizes and capabilities, some conservative, some progressive, some in small towns, and others in good–sized cities, the newsletter can foster a feeling of identity and common purpose among the members, many of whom will not ordinarily come into contact with one another, except at annual meetings and perhaps not

The Metropolitan Library   43 even then. This is crucial to the unity of the system. So, when one library is having a special program that others might want to imitate or adapt, a description should be included in the newsletter. Time, date, and type of activity, however, are not enough. Specifics such as costs, kind of publicity, sponsors, and methods of operation should also be included. Librarians planning new buildings want to know about floor arrangements, color schemes, and unusual facilities of other new buildings already in operation. People are also interested in other people (and in themselves). The mentioning of the names of individuals in the region is a surefire way of involving the members: librarians, trustees, and staff as well.

Again, the use of clear illustrations, good paper stock, color, and careful printing (not mimeograph) can make for an attractive information bulletin that will be read, and just as important, that the member libraries will want to contribute to. (The prevalence of the latter is a good indication of the success of the publication!)

Reading lists, bookmarks, and posters for all age groups can be distributed to the member libraries. These should bear the imprint of the regional system rather than just the headquarters library. On posters and display materials space can be left for the member library to add its name and address.

The number of publications to be sent to each member library ought to be determined by the library itself. Once a survey has been taken (and it should be updated about every three years or as often as circumstances warrant), the totals can be kept on file and when a list is published the requested number will automatically be sent. Special publications such as posters can be advertised separately in the newsletter and asked for separately.

Member libraries should be encouraged to distribute the publications in the ways already discussed. The potential benefits may not be obvious to the library that has never had any of its own and should be referred to as often as necessary!

Because the reading lists will probably be compiled by committees in the headquarters library, these groups should include

Edward J. Montana, Jr.

participants from other parts of the region. In this way the lists, bookmarks, and other materials will have a better balance, regionally speaking, both with regard to subjects and entries. The regional system can also print general lists compiled entirely by the staff of a member library when the subject warrants it.

Public relations workshops may be held. In a smaller region where the membership is fairly homogeneous one per year would be sufficient, but in large areas, a series might be needed, one for each geographical subdivision. Because their problems and challenges are different, a session especially planned for the larger libraries might be in order.

The subjects of the workshops depend on what the member libraries have already been doing in the area of public relations, but starting off with a general introduction and with basic information on using the newspaper and radio and the staging of exhibits would be helpful. Staff members of the radio station and newspaper that the audience will be dealing with may be asked to speak as well as someone from a more advanced library who has done successful PR work. It is a good idea to have a reactor panel to question the speakers. The panelists, from the same areas as the audience, will be able to anticipate and encourage questions from the listeners.

Later sessions may involve a selected number of those who actually do the public relations work in the member libraries and might be a work session on writing newspaper releases and radio spots.

The public relations officer's day–to–day duties in most systems include editing the newsletter, supervising the publications program (including the artwork), planning system–wide public relations workshops, and publicizing the regional system as a whole.

The public relations officer attached to regional headquarters may also be available for consultation by members of the system. The extent of his help is determined by the size of the system and the number of requests. In some systems he will actually plan news releases and spot announcements for a given library, advise on publicity for fund raising and bond issues, and be on call for a reasonable amount of consultation by every library in the system. In others, his advice will be limited to general matters such as the setting up of a radio program as opposed to writing the script and planning the shows, the composing of editorials, e.g., for National Library Week, that can be used by all members, and so on.

A procedures manual for regional use might also be prepared. This booklet should contain something of the history and purpose of the system, the services it provides (and does not provide), the way in which the member library can avail itself of these services, and the responsibilities of the different staff members.

Everything should be spelled out. Taking interlibrary loan as an example, an illustration of the borrowing form should be included, with clear, precise instructions as to how it should be completed. Mention should be made of the classes of items that once lent may be used only in the borrowing library and may not be taken to the patron's home. Length of borrowing period, method of return, responsibility for the material, whether it may be renewed, should all be covered in detail. If the headquarters library does not have the item, but can request it from, e.g., a university or special library if necessary, this should be explained as should the possibility of photoduplicating periodical articles and other materials which do not circulate.

Whether the person who does the public relations work for the headquarters library is the same as the one who handles regional PR would depend on the size of the regional system, its administrative structure, and the relation of the headquarters library to the regional system as a whole. Any decision would have to be based on an analysis of all these elements.

Public relations is more art than science. There are a few basic rules, e.g., concerning the actual writing of a release or the staging of a television program, but these simply involve correct procedure. The what and the when can only be determined by individual circumstances and the experience of those who are supervising the program. Knowing your public is vitally impor-

Edward J. Montana, Jr.

tant. A program that was an instant success in one city could be a disaster in another. And so this chapter has been more concerned with general principles than specific activities. Hopefully, the suggestions have been broad enough so that they can be adapted anywhere.

Notes

1. The "do's and don't's" are reprinted, with permission, from the National Association of Broadcasters' booklet *If You Want Air Time.* The booklet is available from the Association (1771 N Street, N.W., Washington, D.C., 20036). Single copies are free; additional copies are fifteen cents each.

2. Approximately 80% of the total population do not use the public library. Of the 20% that do, 50% (47.1% to be exact) are between the ages of 12 and 21. (22.4% between 12 and 16; 24.9% between 17 and 21.) For the 20% figure, see Robert D. Leigh, *The Public Library in the United States* (New York: Columbia University Press, 1950), p. 31; the other percentages can be found in Charles M. Tiebout and Robert J. Willis, "The Public Nature of Libraries," in *The Public Library and the City*, edited by Ralph W. Conant (Cambridge, Mass.: M.I.T. Press, 1965), pp. 97–98. That the situation has not changed in the twenty years between the Leigh book and the present is evident from Mary Lee Bundy, "Metropolitan Public Library Use," *Wilson Library Bulletin*, 41 (May 1967), 950–961; Mary Lee Bundy, "Factors Influencing Public Library Use," *Wilson Library Bulletin*, 42 (December 1967), pp. 371–382; and William R. Monat, "The Community Library, Its Search for a Vital Purpose," *ALA Bulletin*, 61 (December 1967), p. 1309.

Additional sources that cover library use as well as borrowing are Joseph L. Wheeler, "Top Priority for Cataloging–in–Source," *Library Journal*, 94 (September 15, 1969), p. 3007; and Margaret A. Edwards, "The Fair Garden and the Swarm of Beasts," *Library Journal*, 90 (September 1, 1965), p. 3380.

3. Tiebout and Willis, p. 97–98, "Evidently, 75 percent of society seems willing to subsidize the 1.8 percent of society which dominates the use of libraries, because they believe libraries are good for people—especially other people."

4. See, for example, Robert W. Rodger, "Borrowing Department Store Techniques to Promote Library Service," *Wilson Library Bulletin*, 42 (November 1967), pp. 304–308.

3

Public Relations in a Cooperative Suburban Library System

Gloria Glaser

Gloria Glaser is Public Relations Director, Nassau Library System, Garden City, New York. She is a former editor of the Westbury (N.Y.) *Times* and a former trustee of the Westbury Memorial Library. She is a member of the Publications Committee of the American Library Association's Trustees' Association. Mrs. Glaser holds degrees from Hunter College and from Teachers College, Columbia University.

Public relations on a cooperative system level is often paradoxical. Although the aim of keeping the library image before the public is constant, the area of emphasis within the System varies. Because a cooperative system is one where the System is a library's library—created to serve its autonomous member libraries—the public relations role in promoting the System name and image shifts with changing goals and objectives.

Almost twelve years ago, in 1961, the Nassau Library System was formed. Thirty-two libraries in the County recognized the need for a system and petitioned the state for a charter to establish one. The 1970 "Profile of the Nassau Library System" states, "At that time, the urgency to keep up with the growth in human knowledge, plus the ever-mounting pressure of rising taxes were contributing factors which resulted in this cooperative effort by the libraries. No one library could hope to offer the variety of library services that would be needed. With the organization of a system, local effort would be supplemented and enriched to guarantee quality library service. The local library would maintain its individual autonomy since no system control would be exercised over local library operations."

When the charter was granted and a new Service Center was established, the prime role of the Public Relations Office was to familiarize the general public with this new concept and the name of the System. From the beginning, cordial and close relationships were established with the press. Speaking engagements before community groups crowded the calendar of the Public Relations Consultant. The symbol of the System, a torch with the Nassau Library System name, appeared on decals on library doors; it was seen in posters on library circulation desks and on booklists distributed to the public. A 16mm film describing the System's services was produced and made available for community showings.

As the Nassau Library System continued to grow, there was a public relations de-emphasis on the System itself, with a growing focus on publicizing library service in individual communities. Today, the System message is more subliminal. It is not so much what the System *is* but what it *does* for the individual patron. Publicizing the extended services provided by the System through the local library—e.g., films, direct access, interloan, exhibits, large-print books and talking books—makes the public aware of Nassau Library System services.

At the present time the Nassau Library System is composed of 53 member libraries and a service center. The Public Relations Office serves two publics—an external one and an internal one.

External

The 53 individual libraries of the Nassau Library System differ in size, book and non-book collections, staff, philosophy, and community makeup. And their directors and boards are varied too. They have separate needs, yet they all share a common need: the need to foster good community relationships to insure support and commitment. Within the limits of staff time and personnel, it is the challenge of the Public Relations Office to be called upon for assistance when individual or mutual library needs arise.

I. Individualized Aid

A. Budget and Bond Issue Support

In a time of the tightening tax dollar, Nassau County libraries—most of which must get voter approval on budgets every year—need more than ever to communicate clearly and convincingly with their public to win a "yes" vote. When expansions or new buildings are put up for approval, a planned public relations campaign does much to prepare for a positive community climate. Individual library directors or boards often turn to this office for help in soliciting budget or bond issue support. This consultative help may take any number of forms, such as:

1. Organizing a "Friends of the Library" to promote the library cause

"How to Organize a Friends of the Library," from the Sarah Leslie Wallace book, *Friends of the Library*, ALA,

Gloria Glaser

Chicago, 1962, is a well–plotted chapter that offers clear-cut steps of organization to any fledgling friends group.

2. Using a synchronized slide–tape presentation with many community groups before a budget vote

New devices, such as synchronized slide–tape machines, offer an inexpensive way for the library to saturate a community with the library story. A slide–tape presentation is inexpensive to produce; usually one or more camera buffs can be found on a library staff to take pictures; someone with a pleasant speaking voice can read a simple script for taping. The finished product—although no Hollywood three–dimensional creation—can be disarming and informational. The task of accompanying such a pre–packaged program can be divided among knowledgeable library staffers, trustees, and friends. More program engagements can be filled in more locations using less manpower with this one technique.

3. Planning an open hearing on a building expansion

4. Preparing an annual budget brochure for district mailing

5. Plotting an overall public relations program for year-round planning or for a specific purpose

B. Library Literature

The printed word is a viable means of reaching a broad public, particularly at budget time. Since the public's eye is sated and saturated with advertising forms, the library message must compete with the other forms of printed matter directed to the same audience. A library mailer need not be costly, but it must be competitive for effectiveness. Each year, at our Public Relations Office, help is given to several individual libraries in planning and executing budget mailers customized to their community.

General informational brochures are also developed here at individual requests. One such brochure was used as a prototype for other libraries. Its cover message is "Welcome. Your Card is

Your Key to the——Public Library." Inside the folder, the content includes information on the major services of the library. It is a conventional pamphlet, yet the universal symbol of a key, in a distinctive design created by the staff artist, was so successful that it also served as a springboard for posters and shopping bags made available to all the libraries.

The forms of original library literature most requested from our office by libraries include: letterheads, covers for community directories, newsletter formats, bookmarks, brochures, flyers, and invitations.

C. Consultant Visits

Routine visits to the libraries are part of a year–round effort by the Public Relations Consultant. These visits serve as a two–way communications platform. They offer a get–acquainted opportunity and a chance to exchange public relations views.

When a specific problem arises, the Public Relations Consultant meets with the library director and/or the board of trustees. Quite often, a team of two or more System specialists–consultants, the Director, an Assistant Director visit library boards upon request.

There are times when the telephone visit is the speediest way to resolve a point. Hardly a day goes by when there are not two or more phone calls from directors with a range of questions from, "Where do I purchase a clever but inexpensive giveaway for our open house?" to "Can you arrange for the Long Island Railroad to allow me to put up library posters at our railroad station?"

D. Press and Media Contact

Nassau County is a collection of small communities, and community news is best handled through the local weekly newspaper. More than 70 such local organs exist for the purpose of printing the home town news. Except for the unique feature story or the provocative program of widespread interest, when news is sent to the two Long Island dailies, the local library is encouraged by this office to maintain regular contact with its

Gloria Glaser

community paper. Library news, if clearly written and timely, will get consistent coverage if harmonious relations have been established with the local editor.

Throughout the year, for specific purposes, the Nassau Library System Public Relations Office produces "canned releases" for its libraries. All the member library has to do with such a release is to retype, filling in the appropriate blanks and send it on to its newspaper.

A sample release follows:

The Nassau Library System

TO: Member Library Directors
      Suggested News Release for Weekly Papers

        February 8, 1971   For IMMEDIATE RELEASE

                              Date _____

The opportunity for paid summertime employment in library work is available again this year for college juniors who qualify as library cadets, according to _____ , Director of the _____ Library.

The 1971 federally funded library cadet program, recently announced by Library Futures for the fourth consecutive year, will run from June 21 to August 13. Intended for junior-year college students without career commitments, this recruitment program seeks involvement of the cadets in the diversified services and activities of today's libraries.

The Nassau Library System, the cooperative system for the 53 public libraries of Nassau County, is one of six metropolitan systems participating in the Library Futures Cadet Program.

Cadets will earn $100 per week for a 35-hour week. To qualify, students must be permanent residents of New York

State, enrolled in college full time, completing their junior year by June of 1971 and graduating in 1972. They should be able to commute to work locations in Nassau and Suffolk Counties or other points in the metropolitan area.

April 16 is the deadline for applications and interviews by Library Futures. Application blanks and further details are available from _____ Library.

The effectiveness of this release which appeared in a good many community newspapers each year the program has been operative is evidenced by the record number of applicants for cadet positions in the four years of the cadet program.

Coordinated news and calendar items for member libraries are best handled centrally through this office for radio and television coverage, as well as for monthly reports to *Bookmark*, the New York State library publication.

II. General Help

A. National Library Week

In Nassau County, the promotion of National Library Week serves to highlight the year–round services of all the libraries in the county, as well as to create a climate of good will toward libraries in the critical period of budget presentations.

Each year, the Nassau Library System Public Relations Office joins forces with the Nassau County Library Association in a special National Library Week promotional effort. Plans for National Library Week usually start several months before the April date.

Since 1970 was the year of the library building boom in Nassau County, it seemed natural to use new or renovated buildings as our theme. Six libraries were in various stages of getting settled into new quarters or in additions to original buildings. A

Gloria Glaser

school bus was hired for a "Follow the Yellow Bus Trail" program. This tour was designed to accommodate trustees and Friends of the libraries on Nassau Library Day. It was an opportunity to visit four of the libraries for a personalized tour, with time for questions and comments on costs, design, and new developments in library architecture and furnishings.

The National Library Week focus was quite different for 1971. It was decided to reach out to the non–library user and to involve public, private, school, and special libraries in the effort. Roosevelt Field, the largest shopping center in Nassau County (and incidentally, the home of the Nassau Library System) was chosen as the site and eight areas of presentation and activities were set up on the mall for one day, Nassau Library Day. Saturday shoppers were exposed to booths grouped as: Film Center; Library Services for the Blind, the Homebound, and the Handicapped; Storytelling Theater; Special Materials; Geographic Presentation; Creative Activities; Underground Spin-off and Information Services.

Clear, sunny weather heralded the arrival of April 17—Nassau Library Day. After nine months of intensive preparation —endless committee meetings, communications, planning publicity and printing production—we were on stage. Shoppers on the mall could view award–winning amateur films, get their fortunes told by tarot card, receive print–outs of *The New York Times*, and win prizes in a free raffle drawing. During this all–day program the passerby could also choose a variety of bookmarks to take home, see a rap session with teen authors, savor frying–pan cooking, observe a karate demonstration, or find materials for the handicapped, the blind and the homebound.

Evaluations of the event are still being tabulated. Reports already compiled point out that this form of library persuasion has a place in the competitive bid for the attention of the voter. The reports also show a strengthening of cooperative effort among all types of libraries in the county.

In addition, a highly anticipated yearly event planned for National Library Week is a literary love–in called the *Newsday* Book–Author Luncheon. It is sponsored by the newspaper in cooperation with the Nassau Library System, the Suffolk Library System, and the Nassau County Library Association. More than a thousand people, including library personnel, turn out for the event. The lure and exposure to live authors like Erich Segal and Kate Millet seems to have residual benefits in book sales and library circulation figures.

B. Exhibits

To attract more people to their premises, the libraries of today must use a number of techniques to make their surroundings more inviting. Newer libraries are including display space and showcase areas in their planning; older libraries by judicious rearranging can find wall and shelf space for displays. A growing responsibility of this office has been to provide circulating displays for the county libraries to stimulate interest in the books and non-book materials available for borrowing. Kate Coplan expresses a guideline for exhibits in the chapter, "Some Thoughts on Library Public Relations" from *The Library Reaches Out*, compiled and edited by Kate Coplan and Edwin Castagna, Oceana Publications, 1965:

> But having said that library displays must be attractive, a word of caution against "extremism" may be in order. There is sometimes the danger of becoming too "arty." Attractiveness alone is not enough. It must be remembered that the purpose of the exhibit always is to "sell" the books and information projected to viewers. The librarian can sometimes create a pretty picture, one which is a feast for the eyes, in fact, but it may not motivate sufficient reader interest to request the material presented. In this case, the display has failed of its purpose.

At the present time, we send around some twenty-one exhibits for either wall or showcase display. Some of the new sights on the scene at community libraries in Nassau are copies of etchings by old masters, nineteenth and twentieth century poster art, primitive musical instruments and prizewinning newspaper photos. New exhibits are always in the making. Final arrangements have just been made with the office of State Senator John R. Dunne for this office to circulate a collection of twelve paintings, "Corrections on Canvas." The artists are state penitentiary inmates.

Exhibits from this Public Relations Office to member libraries are ever increasing in scope. Cooperation with outside agencies such as *Newsday*, the Nassau County Museum, and the Long Island Craftsman's Guild have developed exhibits of more than routine interest. When time is available, the assistant to the Public Relations Consultant makes field trips to the libraries using our exhibits to help set up exhibits and to gather information on future display needs of the libraries.

To give further help to libraries seeking new exhibit materials, a booklet entitled *Library Hang-ups*, first produced by this office in 1969, contains a list of exhibits available through the Nassau Library System and from other sources. Included is information on one-man shows by Long Island artists and suggested P/R readings.

C. Workshops

1. Public Relations

In-service training in public relations is wanted and welcomed in Nassau County. Even though several of our libraries employ public relations specialists on a full or a part-time basis, in many cases it is either the library director or a member of the regular staff who is responsible for the public relations assignments in addition to her own work.

In the planning of such workshops, the member library P/R specialists are generous with their time and serve as committee members and program participants. The most recent workshop, an all-day event, stimulated a large turnout and a good representation from the fifty-three libraries to hear a guest expert on library posters, their preparation, and their distribution; the staff artist's slide-talk on "How to Prepare Camera-Ready Art"; and a sensitivity specialist probing "Do You Turn the Public On or

A Cooperative Suburban Library System   59

Off?" A proposed fall workshop, by popular demand, with the staff artist presiding over a "do–it–yourself" paste and scissors session, is a natural outgrowth of the earlier "How–To" program.

2. Friends of the Library

There has been a resurgence of interest in Friends of the Library groups in this area. Thirty of the fifty-three libraries have such groups. Overcoming the lack of communication and exchange of ideas with other such organizations are major areas of interest where the Service Center Public Relations Office can be helpful.

These are some of their questions:

What are the advantages of incorporation?
What successful year–round programs have you had?
Do you charge dues? If so, how much?
Have you ever organized a Junior Friends?
Do you fundraise? How?
Do you publish a newsletter?

In the fall, under the guidance of the Nassau Library System's Public Relations Department, the first Friends forum in a number of years was held. To give the audience background and perspective, the first Public Relations Director of the Nassau Library System was invited as the keynote speaker. A lively panel discussion followed the speech, touching upon such topics as "How to Organize a Friends of the Library," "How NOT to Organize a Friends of the Library," "Junior Friends," "Successful Programs," and "Getting Out a Yes Vote."

There is every indication that there is a genuine need for such groups to continue to keep in touch and have the opportunity of learning from each other's experiences.

III. Unserved Areas

A. The Legally Unserved

In a county such as Nassau, where public library service is not mandated, there are areas where people are unserved be-

Gloria Glaser

cause they are not in a library taxed district. Almost 45,000 people in Nassau County live in some thirteen separate pocket areas that have no library taxing authority. This problem is one of continuing responsibility to the System since a primary objective of the System is "to stimulate the development of service in unserved areas." In the past, System staff and trustees have worked with local citizen committees in the establishment of several new public library districts. Currently, a standing committee of member library directors and trustees is at work attempting to resolve this problem. With the aid of a State consultant, they are trying to devise legislation that would enable these pocket areas to have the legal ability to tax themselves.

The Public Relations Consultant is one of the members of the System staff who may be called upon for help by these communities. Help is given in a number of ways:

At the stage where concerted action is taken by a citizen's group for a referendum, a campaign to get out the vote is planned—printed flyers, postcards are designed and produced by the Public Relations Office; a timetable for the plan is devised; committees are formed; publicity is issued; telephone squads are set up; speakers are selected. Such preparation is similar to a good political campaign in its setup.

An active file is kept of people in unserved areas who call or write to the System for future reference and action.

If public relations guidance is needed in specific circumstances, the Public Relations Consultant may serve as coordinator and liaison agent. Recently, in an unserved area, a local committee organized Saturday openings for the school libraries. This office helped them publicize the new service and put them into contact with system–age level specialists for programming ideas.

B. Other Unserved Patrons

The disadvantaged, the aged, the foreign–speaking, the disabled, the homebound, and the blind are people who may also be considered unserved even though they may have legal access to libraries. The System P/R office serves in a backup capacity for the individual libraries and/or the age–level consultants in handling these areas.

One way the Service Center aids the disadvantaged is with the Mini–mobile. The Mini–mobile is a little, summertime, paper-back library van that brings "tall tales, short stories and rear-screen films" to nine disadvantaged communities in Nassau County. It is a joint venture of the Nassau Library System and the Nassau County Department of Parks and Recreation, in its fourth year of operation.

Each year, the Service Center Public Relations staff prepares bookmarks and summer library cards—familiar to previous pa-trons—because of the day–glo pink Mini–mobile symbol on a pale blue background that is carried over from year to year. Flyers, posters, and news releases are other forms of Mini–mobile promotion provided for by this office.

Internal

The role of the Public Relations Office within the Service Center is to implement the goals and objectives of the System as a whole and of each service in particular.

I. Administration

A. Trustee Workshops

Trustees of individual member libraries meet trustees of other libraries on an infrequent basis. Occasionally, they are invited to area meetings structured by their Nassau Library System board representative, and once a year they have the opportunity to join all other Nassau County library trustees at the annual Trust-ees' Meeting. Trustee workshops, sponsored by the System, are planned when a common problem needs exploration and an ex-change of information seems indicated. Involved people, such as most library trustees are, can be counted upon for attendance if what is being offered is meaningful. The Public Relations Office

Gloria Glaser

is occupied in assisting administration and the board in the meticulous step–by–step details that insure a large and interested audience.

A recent controversial and challenging Regents' position paper on Library Service was the impetus for a 1971 spring Trustees' Workshop. Because of the importance of the paper and its implications for the future of library service in New York State, trustees of the adjoining county of Suffolk were also invited. A comprehensive program was structured, and a library site, convenient to both counties was chosen. Plentiful and advance publicity, with telephone follow–up, kept trustees alerted to the event. The appearance of a State Regent on the program, followed by important and informed speakers, netted a filled auditorium on a spring Saturday morning.

B. Legislative Action

Increasing competition for the State tax dollar makes it imperative that legislative action be considered yet another area for public relations involvement on a system level. With the knowledge that cutbacks in state funds were imminent for 1971, New York State library systems, for the first time, made a concerted effort to impress the seriousness of the library financial picture upon the legislators. The Nassau Library System joined in the efforts to get both legislators and constituents to meet in a one–to–one relationship at a March legislative breakfast in Albany, sponsored by the New York Library Association and Library Trustees Foundation. The Public Relations Office assisted in this endeavor as well as in the production and distribution of 10,000 letters of appeal, distributed to trustees, patrons, publishers, Friends, and staff, asking them to write to their legislators in support of library funding.

C. Annual Meeting

Planning for an annual meeting of the Nassau Library System Board of Trustees—with the hope that a maximum number of member library trustees will attend—is a yearly task that requires much effort and thinking through. Because bylaws dic-

A Cooperative Suburban Library System 63

tate that this once–a–year business meeting of the NLS board and member library trustees takes place in January, planning for this event requires the right combination of weather and charismatic circumstances. Once administration and the board of trustees decide the direction the annual meeting will take, the Public Relations Office works out the details. Here is a sample of a news release on the event:

> The January 13, 1971 NLS annual meeting met the rigorous test for success. The excitement of the setting —the newest and most glamorous of Nassau libraries, the Port Washington Library—was a powerful inducement. Added to that, was the prestige of the speakers: guest of honor, John Humphry, Assistant Commissioner for Libraries, New York State; and speaker, Harold Roth, Director of the new Nassau County Reference Library. A cold, clear night, a wine and cheese reception (courtesy of the French Food and Wine Industry), and the warm hospitality of the Friends and the staff of the Port Washington Library added to the enjoyment of the overflow audience that attended.

D. Annual Reports, Newsletters

1. Annual Report

Each year for the edification of a specialized public—trustees, library staff, and legislators—an annual report is issued. It is a cooperative effort involving the gathering of data by department and division heads, with the final format, once approved by the director, under the jurisdiction of the Public Relations Office.

Annual reports, in any given year, present problems of communication. These problems are shared by any organization preparing such a report. A contemporary booklet, "Aunt Jane, the Analyst and a New Look at Annual Reports" by Winthrop C. Neilson and Gerald G. Lind, offers compassionate understanding and a wry sense of humor for future weaponry in the battle of the annual message. In the preface, the following statement

Gloria Glaser

establishes the atmosphere of the contents that follow:

> To our readers: Producing an annual report often involves unique problems. In this last section we have attempted to cover just a few of these. Perhaps our suggestions will ease some embarrassing situations and, at the same time, provide some short cuts to make your life a little more pleasant. (Page 26 discusses, among other things, the question of whether a president should smile or not for his annual report photograph.) We offer this booklet as a guide to you. Good luck in all your future efforts.

Some of the points that are covered in this publication to help "Aunt Jane" get her money's worth out of an annual report include:

The Coordinator	Normally Writing Is Not Fun
Annual Report Diary	False Dates for Getting Material In
The Annual Report Schedule	Design
	Pressure
Last Year's Report	Copy Heavy Text
The Theme	Consistency
The Difficult Director	

2. Newsletters

a. Administrative
Timely information on the ongoing activities of the Service Center is disseminated to trustees, directors, and library staff members of all fifty-three libraries with the issuance of a monthly newsletter, *Library Lines*. It is edited and produced under the supervision of the P/R office.

b. Staff
A weekly staff newsletter helps to keep the more than a hundred employees of the Service Center in contact with each other and with what is going on at the Service Center.

A Cooperative Suburban Library System 65

II. Programs and Services

Nassau Library System consultants—Adult Services, Young Adult Services, Children's Services, Audio Visual, and Reference —call upon the Public Relations Office for a variety of production needs. From editorial expertise to coffee and name tags, with a good deal of bulk publication in between, certain recurring patterns of service, which take up a major portion of staff time, are performed for the consultants.

One example of the scope and quantity of certain production assignments is the yearly Summer Reading Club, a responsibility of the Children's Services Division:

Public Relations Production Schedule for 1971 Summer Reading Club
    Theme–Slogan:
    Wheeling Along With Books. (The emphasis is on the evolution of the wheel, from its crude beginnings to future uses.)
    Materials to be furnished to participating libraries:

1. *Outline Map* (50)—Large, free standing, attractively designed. It is clearly marked and constructed of material which will facilitate the insertion of pins. Each child will be able to easily follow his reading progress with the use of his wheel models.
2. *Posters* (500)—14″ × 17″—announcing the club. Each poster will include the design, slogan and the words "Join the Summer Reading Club." Adequate space will be provided for the library's name and starting date. These posters may be placed in the library, schools, business, community agencies, etc.
3. *Wheel Models* (15,000)—(approximately 1″ × 1½″) suitable for plotting on the map with the name of the reader on it.
4. *Bookmarks with slogan* (15,000)—Blank spaces provided for each library to add its registration deadline.
5. *Record Card with slogan* (12,000)—Space provided for child's name, address, school, phone number, and

         Gloria Glaser

book titles. Printed on stock suitable for filing.
6. *Certificates* (12,000)—To be issued upon completion of the program.
7. *Booklists* (15,000)—Listing titles in three categories (J-E, middle grades, older readers) which may serve as suggested reading in conjunction with the reading club and for children not in the club.

Other production requests run the gamut from special publications (such as "Library Yardstick, a Self-Study Questionnaire"), booklists, the young adult magazine *Scrutinize*, film catalogs, posters, bookmarks to workshop assistance (invitations, press releases, photo coverage).

Summary

In the preceding pages I have attempted to demonstrate that the constant aim of the Public Relations Office of the Nassau Library System is to keep the library image before the public but that the role of public relations in this cooperative system shifts with changing goals and objectives.

At the Service Center cordial and close relationships with the press continue and new media contacts are pursued. Cooperation with county agencies, through the Service Center staff, as well as through personal contact, grows with the years. New technological tools are used for competitive marketing of our "product." Yet with all the multi–media advances and the abundance of professional gadgetry that may be employed, the essence of good library public relations at the Nassau Library System is the promotion of good library service all year round.

4

Public Relations in the Small Public Library

Wessie Connell

Wessie Connell has been librarian of the Roddenberry Memorial Library, the public library of Cairo, Georgia (Pop.: 8,100) since 1939. The library received John Cotton Dana awards in 1948, 1949, 1958, and 1959.

The very concept of a free library is freighted with the responsibility to see that the public is aware of its availability and cognizant of its contents as it relates to them. The rapid transition, social and political, in recent years faced not only by our society as a whole, but by individuals adds impetus to our performance, and a sense of urgency in evaluating our role and placing priorities on services. We find social patterns disintegrating, value systems in sharp conflict, young people searching and seeking for identity, vocally and physically expressed dissidence—all these strain the fabric of traditional approaches toward publicizing library resources.

A public that seeks to escape from tension, boredom, overwork, too much leisure, a consuming desire for "creature comforts" (by those deprived of them), and an abandonment of complacency (by those satiated with materialism) offers the library the true opportunity to be the catalytic community force.

One recognizes that a library is a service, not merely a handsome building, although that enhances service and offers community pride. Libraries are more than collections of books, catalogued and in the custody of trained personnel; libraries are viable things, nurtured from within by knowledgeable staff and given vigor and stimuli by those who use them.

Any public relations program is concerned with a variety of approaches. The philosophy relating to public relations in a small library is as goal–oriented as the philosophy of a specialist in a library serving an urban area. We, too, have our segmented publics—the ghetto, the affluent and the in-betweens. However, our advantage rests with constant close observation as programs overlap and an entire community reflects in certain tangible forms the impact of specific projects.

Public relations serves as an umbrella to cover all of the publicity programs of libraries, because public relations always exists whether good or bad. You can't decide whether to have a public relations program—your responsibility is to decide what kind of program your library will have. Public relations is an act of public behavior. The professionals might say, "You've got to tell them to sell them."

A public relations program cannot be turned on and off at will, like a faucet or like a publicity program, with which it is so often confused. A public relations program in a library is organized. In our handbook of policies and procedures, a chapter lists planned activities by the month, with notations for those programs held on a yearly basis. This schedule is flexible. We use all media, knowing the wide scope of an encompassing program needs imagination.

Abraham Lincoln commented that public sentiment meant everything. With it nothing can fail, and without it nothing can succeed. We agree, and therefore at close range we evaluate where success lies, and we study the programs that reach to the heart of people. Realistic thinking tells us it is the lack of the personal touch and the denial of the recognition of the individual that has been the Achilles heel of our society and created polarization of groups and individuals. To reach the inner person we experiment and use every medium.

All programs use printed brochures, annotated bibliographies, annual reports, TV shows, radio reviews and announcements, discussion groups, book talks, as a part of a total plan.

Libraries are not always service oriented, but hosts of librarians recognize the worth of the product that they are selling—ideas. In some libraries books are selected and processed, but little effort is made to introduce a collection to the very people the books were chosen to serve. Ideas can be found in all the resources of a library, whether those resources are books, the traditional media leading to knowledge, or art, audio, or visual. Our role is not to be the do–gooder, but what is wrong if that is a by-product?

Our role is varied and our institutions vary in philosophy and in assigning priorities. Small towns are no longer isolated, as individuals take the same packaged travel tours, subscribe to the same magazines, join the same book clubs, read the same best sellers, and are mesmerized by the same TV shows. Our people in this small town range from the illiterate to the highly sophisticated, from the lowest economic level to great wealth.

Primarily our programs are tempered by our background and

Wessie Connell

our institutional needs as reflected by the fragmented publics that we serve. But responsiveness to a community where roots lie deeply has influenced our plans. Projects may be limited from lack of monies but dreams are not denied.

Although the library's supportive role toward education undergirds many of our programs, our responsibility is to those out of school—the uneducated and the disadvantaged (economically, socially, and spiritually). We are trying to reach not one public, but many publics, comprising individuals with idiosyncracies, with prejudices, linked together by the common denominator of man's loneliness and his search for his own identity.

We are concerned that the library's voice be heard by the people of today: the migrant worker, the slow learner, the drug addict—all need us; and the scholar must be served as well as the disadvantaged student. The reader in the small town must be told that through networks of service, no library is isolated, that the resources of all libraries are available through interlibrary loans. Recognition of the variety of patrons is part of the basic premise of a library service.

The basics of a successful program depend on a climate that is generated by the people who comprise the library staff and the board of trustees. Librarians should use their boards not only for policy making, but should listen to their opinions, as they reflect community attitudes. Monthly meetings of the library board of trustees create a sound climate conducive to experimental programs, and offer the librarian the benefit of guidance by a group of responsible adults.

Library boards also talk to their peers in the community. The better informed they are of the library's aims and programs, the more enthusiastic they are in imparting this information to others. Involvement of board members can include presentation of certificates at Book Week programs, and help with children's programs, such as Animal Fairs, and acting as hosts for group services. Board members serve as a part of the total public relations program of the community.

Board meetings offer an opportunity to evaluate a service, with a board member reporting on the program, rather than the librarian. In our community, usually a man hosts coffees and seminars for business groups, and a woman on the board serves as hostess to garden club groups. Their comments give the librarian insight into service.

A sound public relations program, like charity, begins at home, and staff members who feel that they are an important part of a worthwhile activity are able to identify with the creation of a specific program. What a staff member thinks, he speaks to his family, to his neighbors, and to a widening group of friends. Belief in what one is doing is essential. All staff members, with their varied backgrounds, serve, too, as sounding boards for ideas. Library staff members, through staff meetings and coffee breaks, have time to dissect a projected activity; the end is not mere cooperation but coordination of the programs.

An entire project has been scrapped or postponed because a staff member felt that the timing was bad or expressed apathy, an attitude that could permeate the attitude of others. In a small town, a program must be everybody's business if it is to be successful.

I would suggest that directors in choosing staff members should look for attributes that lend themselves to the institution's purpose. In a small town there is great opportunity to screen and evaluate before hiring. Qualities not easily catalogued or listed in a job resume can be observed. New staff members are encouraged to read *A History of the Cairo Public Library*, which was a paper written by Barbara Chapman Williams as partial fulfillment for a degree of Master of Science at Florida State University. This enables them to understand the changes in the times and note the undertones of economic and political behavior as reflected in library progress. The handbook of job descriptions is also suggested reading for understanding the myriad duties of other staff members and to see the employees work as a whole in creating an institution whose raison d'être is service. What the janitor says on the street is just as important to his peer group as what the reference librarian says in a prepared speech to members of a Rotary Club.

From our library's beginning in 1939, to set the climate of

Wessie Connell

public acceptance, many requests have been honored that were not reference questions in a literal sense, to put it mildly. The question from a stout lady, asking for a size forty-four coat pattern, momentarily shocked me until I recalled that she was a member of a home demonstration group where I had recently spoken. Another stout lady lent me size forty-four pattern, resulting in a satisfied patron who never realized her request was not usual and a library friend who had something to share—a size forty-four coat pattern. A second question, similar in its incongruity, came from a tobacco farmer, who asked the selling price of tobacco in a market some distance away and the time he could make delivery. He was advised politely that this was a public library, and he gave a logical reason for coming to the library—we could answer his questions. We called the tobacco auctioneer and got the answers. The result—a satisfied farmer, later an ardent library patron, who used his voice and influence on boards where decisions were important to library development. This was a basic lesson in satisfying the patron and answering rather than questioning the questioner. To sell a service, one often begins with selling himself and proving his sincerity to serve.

The changes that have occurred in the South have been overwhelming and this small public library has been credited with the smooth transition of integration in this community. The library took the initiative where church leaders often were timorous and political figures dared not challenge the accepted mores of the community. The library was never a segregated institution; everyone was encouraged to become all he could be; no one has ever been denied the knowledge found in books. Laubach's theory, "Each one teach one," was indelibly impressed on me when I spoke to a Negro PTA in the early forties. After my talk, a discussion on what reading could do for the child prompted a teacher in the group to speak out. With natural dignity, she explained that her parents were denied an education but her mother was a good student. Each day when the children returned from school, the mother asked what they had learned that day. Her father never asked them. In a quiet voice the teacher added, "He didn't ask us, he asked our mama." Our library opened a special branch in a thickly populated Negro community to enable small school children to share the excitement of a library as a place of involvement.

Receptions there for senior students and their parents have brought many of the parents into the library for the first time. Concerts unite all music lovers, and public speakers elicit the interests of the educated Negro. Because of the dearth of good Negro material in years past, in–service training programs for staff often dwelt on the scarcity of Negro literature. We noted that the self–image of the Negro was marred when a child asked for information on a member of his race, one who had made a contribution to society, and little material was available in the library.

To give dignity to an individual is to use the strongest weapon that one has. Our methods are adapted to suit the individual community. Everyone has a part in helping to ameliorate one of society's most enervating ills. I suggest librarians concentrate their attention on needs of these groups; the implication of the insensitivity of professionals to society's weakness will eventually undermine the core of our institutions.

Now, reputable publishers are publishing books on minority groups, helping the white reader in the South to gain an insight into the struggle of the black race and to learn to respect its contributions to history and society. The Negro is not denied knowledge of the accomplishments of his race and can hold his head higher.

Some of the methods and programs that we have used to reach the Negro community have been less sophisticated than those used for the white community, because of lower incomes and lower educational levels. This is changing at a rapid rate. To make the child feel comfortable, to give that child a sense of respect for himself, was to strengthen his own willingness and own desire to obtain an education. To schedule displays of art work by minority groups (the Negro and the migratory worker) has been a part of a two–way street. To have them participate in

Wessie Connell

programs has lent them dignity and afforded pleasure for everyone.

It has been the library's concern, their challenge, their obligation, coupled with a commitment to serve all people, that has accounted for acceptance by both races. Negro staff members have always been a part of the growth of the library and have strengthened the respect of the white library patrons for the Negro. In turn the Negro staff members have been able to interpret the programs and possibly the attitude of the staff and of the library to their own people. There have been inequities, injustices, and yet, little by little, books added to the collection (plus excellent magazines on the black race) have helped each race understand the position of members of another group.

After thirty years as a librarian, I can say that it is also a good time to be a librarian if one continues to have faith in the power of the printed word, if one continues to believe that man carries within him the seed of greatness. Books are important and ideas are powerful. When dictators demand their burning and demagogues threaten to close libraries if certain titles are included on the shelves, librarians have an added responsibility to publicize and to use all means of emphasizing learning and knowledge in sharing and molding individual lives.

Censorship and intellectual freedom concern the librarian of today. And the invasion of an individual's right and the protection of his privacy regarding what he reads are basic to intellectual freedom. However, it seems that at times librarians assume a "holier than thou" role and do not take the community into their confidence in demonstrating that it is their obligation and their privilege to choose titles of books on both sides of any controversial issue. When librarians flatly refuse to change positions and boards become involved over titles that have been singled out by individuals, a little diplomacy, tact, and understanding can resolve the situation before it gets out of hand. There is no area in the library field that is more important than establishing a climate of trust so that the community can feel confident that when a book is chosen and material is acquired with tax money or with gifts, it is chosen out of concern for the individual and the development of his power to reason.

All libraries have policies concerning the acceptance of books, magazines, and other materials as gifts. We accept anything that is given the library, with the proviso that the librarians use their judgment as to how, when, and where such material is used. I overheard the haughty tone of a staff member in a library answering a patron who had offered old books to the library, "We don't accept used books of any kind." I noted the look of dejection and defeat on the face of the would-be giver and recognized the impoverishment of the library that did not welcome gifts, although they might attach strings to their use.

The library's relationship with the press is a two-way street, and we attempt to merit their support. In essence, we go the extra mile and initiate activities which engender good will with our newspaper. For example, we furnish extra columns or fillers not merely on library news but on things of interest to the entire area. When the annual Rattlesnake Round-Up is held in a neighboring community in February, the editor is furnished a fact sheet on snakes by the library, and in the fall during the hurricane season fact sheets on weather and cyclones are furnished the paper. Occasionally we list titles of relevant books.

A weekly column in the only local newspaper, "Your Public Library is Yours—Use It," runs the gamut from lists of best sellers to articles philosophizing on subjects as varied as ecology, the feminist movement, sex education, and camping. Items that are significant and that are in the news are commented on in the library column, with book lists appropriate to the subject mentioned. For instance, seasonal columns at camellia show time feature books on gardening and the camellia; the season of Lent offers an opportunity to list religious books; and book annotations on home and family relations at Four-H Club Week. Community, state, and national events can be tied in with the regular column, listing books as background reading.

We count this as killing two birds with one stone, helping build good will and serendipitous service to the library. Names

Wessie Connell

(numbering as many as five hundred) of boys and girls who have read books in the summer reading program are listed by the paper during the Christmas season when a larger edition is printed and the paper needs copy.

The local radio station welcomes spot announcements, with spots used frequently throughout the day. Items of interest and fillers are sent regularly to the radio news editor. They, too, have relevance and we attempt to slant spots for the rock music program with young adult happenings; the same philosophy applies to spots listing books to follow the devotional programs of the station. Radio remains a powerful tool, as people are tuned in while shaving, while driving to and from work, when stalled in traffic jams. For many years the library has reached non-readers and readers alike through the Saturday morning Pied Piper Story Hour, with stories told by staff members and by speech majors during summer vacations. This program was started in 1948, and letters to the library verify that it is still listened to with interest.

At the end of the summer when school starts and we approach Book Week time, principals are alerted to put the dates on their calendar so that teachers in the school can make plans early. Editorials in the paper and over the TV station and over radio underscore the library's activities for Book Week.

Children's Book Week includes special displays of proclamations issued by mayors since the library began in 1939 and resolutions by Chairmen of the County Boards of Roads and Revenues. The current proclamation, signed by the mayor and placed in the paper and prominently displayed in the library, interests older library patrons. Programs in the schools are a big part of a child's life, and newspaper coverage is good, with pictures of participants and programs encouraging teachers to go all out in staging dramatic shows. Parents attend and dignitaries present the certificates. This is another time that library board members take an active part.

Book Week teas have honored local authors during Book Week and at other times retired teachers have been similarly honored. Special art work by the children carrying out the theme with poster contests have also been a part of Book Week activities.

Special weeks of the year such as National Library Week elicit editorials and business firms, including banks, are asked to use the library slogan in their ads.

Scrapbooks of library activities, composed of newspaper clippings, pictures, and brochures, are prepared each year. A member of the community chosen by library staff members is honored by having the year's service dedicated to him or her. It is a prestigious occasion held in the library with past recipients and their families and business associates participating in the presentation ceremony. These names are engraved on a plaque hanging in the foyer of the library and all news media cover the occasion. The scrapbooks remain the property of the library and serve to tell the library's story to visitors and to students of library schools. This award is an annual part of observance of National Book Week.

Our first scrapbook won a John Cotton Dana award, followed by three other John Cotton Dana awards. It is significant that the eminent public relations expert, Edward L. Bernays, served on the first jury. His approval gave a green light to our library to break new ground in publicizing a library service and to merit an award named in honor of a librarian who broke tradition and alerted his community to the fine art of communication. (Incidentally, this award, with others, results in community pride to the extent of securing each year the money requested in our budget.)

Always publicize awards; don't be modest. (I once feared professional jealousy and was hesitant.) A community takes pride in an establishment that receives outside recognition.

Our three sponsoring agencies, i.e., The City of Cairo, County Board of Roads and Revenues, and County Board of Education, who support the library and underwrite it with the tax dollar, offer another avenue to tell and sell: commission members become more enthusiastic for programs they vote to support with the tax dollar. Yearly reports are sent to individual members for perusal and study at their leisure with a personal

Wessie Connell

letter from the librarian, although a copy is always filed with the secretary for permanence. We feel the importance of recognizing each member and keeping him informed regarding programs, projects, and philosophy. We "keep our fences mended" and do not wait until the yearly presentation of the budget to deluge agencies with facts and figures. Copies of brochures are often tucked into letters to members of these agencies. The librarian makes opportunities to appear before the agencies during the year if a new service is started so that members feel informed. Consequently they are more likely to support programs without coercion from the press or public. Members of these agencies are invited to help host special events; they do not always accept, but seem to value the invitation. If they do come, their pictures are placed in the paper and Polaroid shots are always sent to their families. The cost—a little extra time and thought, a few cents for pictures. When did the professional person get the idea that theirs was an eight-hour day?

Libraries sometimes fail to court favor from the groups instrumental to programs and then censor these groups for lack of interest. They win votes at the polls for supporting popular programs, such as the library, and the library wins their confidence as they see where part of their tax dollar goes. Citizens reflecting various professions and business interests are invited to help host such diverse events as coffees for businessmen, teas to welcome teachers at pre–planning groups, and chapel programs to present reading certificates. This participation gives these members of the agencies an opportunity to understand the broader range of the library program.

The guest book of the library offers a subtle means of publicizing the library, as feature stories have appeared in the paper listing names of prominent guests and places of their residence. Often letters have been sent to professional people when the librarian was not present to greet them personally.

Whenever an award is made to an individual in the community, the library arranges a display and publicizes the honor. The City of Cairo won the coveted "Certified City" Award, and a special display was made, with the award prominently displayed in the library. Newspaper coverage was good.

"Thank you" letters always acknowledge any special gift of time, books, flowers, money. Librarians often plead "too busy" for grace notes, but simple courtesies beget larger returns in financial support and increased circulation figures.

The library has often given guidance to groups that already existed by supplementing their institutional offerings. The library works with other community leaders in programs of social and educational significance. We do not have a formal "Friends of the Library," but we have endeavored instead to make the entire community our "friends" by working through organizations with definite goals or by helping to organize groups with similar interests.

Our library in its infancy placed emphasis on two adult groups—both articulate: organized church women's groups and insurance agents. The church groups make contributions of books and money to the religious collection; we recognized that they placed their gifts with their hearts, and these gestures prompted wider use of the religious collection and related collections on social betterment. Pre–planning clinics for vacation Bible school teachers, held each spring in the library with exhibits of books, filmstrips, and maps, resulted in increased circulation and, we hope, more stimulating summer schools. Church groups have helped sponsor Sunday School clinics that were co–sponsored by the Ministerial Association, the latter serving with members of the library board as hosts. The Ministerial Association uses its voice in publicizing library events from the pulpit and in church bulletins.

A personalized form letter (if there is such a thing) is sent to all new ministers in the county. The library cooperates with the Ministerial Association, an ecumenical group, and sponsors special displays called "Religious Books of the Month." Books and magazines are featured in a prominent spot in the library and listed in church bulletins, newspapers, and over the radio. The selection rotates among the churches, and each month a different church makes the selection.

Wessie Connell

Local women's groups cooperate with the Women's Church Clinic, with each denomination having a center featuring material such as devotional aids, program helps, and filmstrips. The project results in a new understanding among denominations and increased use of books on social action, drug use, studies in grief, and other problems. During Lent the library distributes thousands of brochures to all churches. Community Thanksgiving services offer another opportunity to distribute annotated book lists. Noon programs during Lent at the library feature a brief program of music and meditation and are planned by ministerial groups. Window displays feature Bibles of various translations to observe the week. Future plans call for coffee and doughnuts in the court, with youth groups planning Lenten observation for one week, prior to classes. Guitars and banjos will play their kind of music.

For senior citizens we develop programs centering on nutrition, legislation, health care, second careers, and film programs that allow armchair traveling. The diversity of interests is as broad in this group as in other age groups. Weekly programs at a housing project, mainly occupied by the elderly, have brought to our attention many volunteers with much to offer the community. Programs at a nursing home are more limited, but we are learning through trial and error.

The most exciting adult services have come through total integration of the schools. The library's traditional role, supportive of the school program, has grown in depth. Members of the County Board of Education and the County School Superintendent, with the cooperation of the Curriculum Director, welcome and greet teachers to all school affairs. Pre–planning week has involved the library during the first week of school, finding teachers meeting together as groups in the library. With the help of the Curriculum Director, schedules are planned so that all teachers visit the library. Usually a cup of coffee is enjoyed in the librarian's office or on the portico. As an outgrowth, Science Round Tables, Social Studies groups, and English Councils have been formed. These special interest groups meet regularly, and often the program is introduced with the showing of slides of library activities concerning their special interests. Book reviews, evaluation of professional journals, and film previews are part of the activity of such school–oriented groups. We give some credit for the smooth transition of the school system to this totally integrated program, because at these Round Tables teachers meet and discover common problems.

Classroom visits are scheduled. This is an excellent method of publicizing the library, as classes that are within walking distance of the library schedule walking tours. The entire community is aware of the library's involvement with the school. When school buses line the parking lot and classes come on a rotating plan, they dramatize the library's role in education. Staff members frequently invite knowledgeable community members as resource people, if teachers have requested discussion of specific subjects. This saves librarians hours of study and enriches the students.

The portico offers the perfect setting, with a giant oak tree filled with squirrel and bird nests, and a Saint Francis fountain in the background, for storytelling and poetry readings. A hole with a white stone rabbit prompts mention of Alice's visit to Wonderland. A mutilated rock prods us to tell stories of the Indians who were here first. These are stage props, but effective.

At the beginning of the school year all the librarians in the community, including the medical records librarian of the hospital, are invited by the public librarian to meet together. This group is loosely organized, but in working together the library program in the community is strengthened and prestige increases for the profession as a whole.

Art exhibits from the Smithsonian Institution and art exhibits by local artists are held, with teas to which the public is invited. Displays are borrowed from people in the community. Many times the loan of a precious collection of gems or artifacts mark the first visit made by the collector to the library.

Films on golfing are presented to the Women's Golfing Association, with the library staging a coffee hour in their honor. This has increased substantially the use of the collection on sports, and has brought former nonreaders into the library.

Wessie Connell

Librarians appear on TV shows with demonstrations of machines for the handicapped and the blind, appear on panels, discuss new books, including the controversial ones.

A staff member regularly visits the prison camp, the jail, the hospital, and the nursing homes. We convince a community of the library's sincerity in reaching out to people confined to bed or to prison. An experimental program was launched with the help of the County Commissioners in an effort toward rehabilitation. Questionnaires were prepared by the library.

Real estate agents and representatives of the local Chamber of Commerce are encouraged to bring guests (industrial prospects and new residents) for a cup of coffee and a tour of the library. Business appreciates this aspect of publicizing a place of community pride. We try to help sell the community by telling about library programs and emphasizing the cultural side of the community.

Hobby shows offer an opportunity for individuals to display the things that they are interested in most, and the library is afforded a chance to display relevant books.

A genealogy clinic allows those interested in family history to come to the library to hear outstanding speakers. A library staff member reviews books on genealogy and gives a short course on the steps in preparing one's family chart. This frees library members from dealing with individuals and, since it is a prestigious group, the mayor usually welcomes the visitors and guests to the library and board members host the group. It is much publicized over several states.

Preparation of brochures is not complicated in our small library. A typist cuts a stencil and someone with imagination and ingenuity prepares the layout. Brochures and simple bulletins are prepared on a myriad of subjects and distributed to diverse groups. These mimeographed brochures are presented at men's clubs, listing books on hobbies, business, and public affairs. For garden clubs we prepare bibliographies with annotations of planting aids. We admit to a bit of plagiarism at times and give credit when we know the source of our drawings or quotes. Varied interest groups prompt specific bibliographies. If the brochure is professionally printed, it is often dedicated to an individual, with his family bearing the cost of printing. This makes excellent publicity, encouraging others to make gifts, and enables us to have professionally printed lists for special occasions.

Businessmen have a special area set aside known as the Businessmen's Corner. It is supported by a local bank in honor of a former president. Women are excluded from this area so that no patron need interrupt his reading to stand for a lady. Such diverse material as *The Wall Street Journal* and *Playboy* are shelved in this area. All business books and magazines are part of the gift from the bank.

Small Business Aids (free) are on a "Take One" shelf. The library uses the free business aids on a variety of subjects as a means of introducing books on such topics as starting a drug store, opening a beauty parlor, starting a nursery or flower shop. These free government aids from the Small Business Administration are sent to new people in the community, and hopefully this will contribute to raising the economic level of the community. Fliers giving library information have been placed in telephone bills that go to every consumer in the county. The library prepares a brochure that is presented at coffees for businessmen, and is distributed at Rotary Clubs, Lions Clubs, Kiwanis, American Legion, and at any meeting where businessmen gather.

An investment clinic held over a period of several weeks was quite successful and increased the use of business books. We reviewed magazine holdings and explained the use of the *Index to Business Periodicals*. These tools were unfamiliar to most of the group of men and women attending. Introduction to how-to books on reading the stock market has prompted a group of retired businessmen to become regular patrons.

A morning coffee was held, with letters sent to every businessman in the community. The list of names came from listing of owners of city licenses. Specific groups have been brought into the library for talks, usually with ninety percent answering the invitations mailed from the library. The librarian always adds a personal note so that it is not a cut-and-dried form

Wessie Connell

letter. Time consuming, yes—worth it, yes. Lawyers, real estate agents, retail merchants, and insurance salesmen were invited at different times to see library materials of specific interest for their profession. Brochures, prepared with annotations of books, were presented to them.

The gift of memorial books has been a continuing and growing project started thirty years ago, at present accounting for approximately one-fourth of the entire book purchases for the year.

Our most unusual memorial (books, plants, objets d'art are the familiar memorials) is a book honoring the memory of a dog. This was bought with dimes from students in a fifth grade class that shared their teacher's grief at the death of her pet dog, a familiar sight on the school campus. A book by Terhune was appropriately marked with the library's memorial plate.

Subliminal advertising was a part of an annual garden tour of homes in Cairo. We asked permission to place books in these homes, blending with the decor and relating to family interest. The books were not stamped with library ownership, and many bore the original covers. A remark by an out of town visitor was that "she had never seen a town with so much culture." Incidentally, most of the hostesses in the homes requested copies of the books and ordered them for their personal use. We recall that one home, newly built on the edge of a wooded area, prompted the librarian to choose books on birds and place them on a table near a window; a pair of binoculars was also loaned and called attention to the books. Because of this small gesture this family became ardent bird watchers and users of the library's books.

Staff members are trained to watch individuals and note reading preferences in an effort to personalize the service. If pregnancy is obvious, suggestions of books on child care are made.

A Welcome Wagon has helped the library to alert new families in the community to library resources, and the library on several occasions has co-hosted with the Welcome Wagon in sponsoring a party for brides and their mothers. At that time etiquette books were arranged, and brief talks were followed by a tea.

An adult program that was designed to help the Negro, the minority group in this area, become more adept at leadership consisted of Leadership Clinics. A volunteer of the community explained Robert's Rules of Order, and the library distributed bulletins on conducting meetings. This program drew new people into the library. The officers of organized clubs were also invited.

The Rose Show Parade in Thomasville, Georgia, a neighboring town, offered an opportunity to enter a float that we knew would be seen by thousands of spectators and also viewed by TV audiences. An old horse–drawn hearse used at the turn of the century loaned by a local funeral establishment was dramatic—a direct contrast with the flower–bedecked floats carrying beautiful girls. Through the open windows of the hearse one could see a casket covered with red roses. Lettered in black on a large white board was the simple phrase: "The Cairo Public Library announces the Death of Ignorance through Books." In the crowd was a small boy who rushed to his mother and in a tremulous voice cried, "Here comes the stagecoach." We heard an adverse comment to the effect that this note was inappropriate; the picture sent to the *Library Journal* and the congratulatory letters that followed mitigated the criticism.

Booths in the annual County Fair have ranged from a house of cardboard plastered in bookjackets entitled "The House that Jack Built" to slide showings, automatically controlled, of library services. Another year the booth featured a large display of snapshots taken in the library twenty years before captioned "Where were you?"

During the city centennial, the library booth displayed old billboards, posters, blown–up ledgers, medical advice, maps, and corseted ladies reflecting the 1870s. The caption read, "We have the answers now."

Clubs find an open door to the library, with groups discussing table settings, flower arranging, and program planning. The library has sponsored garden club clinics with talks on books, slide shows, and by helping garden club members plan their year's programs. This has encouraged the use of books from our extensive garden collection. It saves staff time to help thirteen clubs plan programs at a joint meeting, and introduces services to groups with individual members returning to browse and borrow. Use of card catalog, vertical file, readers guides can be explained to a group without fear of talking down to those not familiar with these tools. Incidentally, garden clubs pay for all garden periodicals. Garden clubs receive at least three short letters from the library each year—the first sent to the Council advising members of cost of periodicals; the second acknowledging the check; and a third thanking the members for flower arrangements. These letters are little reminders, but reach members of the most active civic club in the area.

Not only has there been wider use of gardening books, but we have received fresh flower arrangements on a regular schedule from the Garden Club Council. A card stands near the flowers giving the arrangers' names and the name of the club. Describing these arrangements for the newspaper in a weekly column, "Flower Notes From Your Library," takes time, but brings visitors in to study the arrangements and perchance to borrow a book. At the end of the year a certificate of merit is presented to the club that has made the most outstanding contribution. The chairman of the Library Board makes the presentation. The club honored has its name engraved on a brass bowl that is the property of the library and is used in some arrangements.

A children's art exhibit held in the spring in our staff parking lot offers a Greenwich Village atmosphere. Parents, art teachers, and the Curriculum Director help arrange the program. The mayor welcomes families, and the grand opening is covered by newspaper, radio, and TV. Categories are broad and the majority of the children leave with some type of ribbon. This is a culmination of the art projects of the school year.

At Christmas the library's annual children's party gives an aura of gaiety to the children's area, beautifully decorated with mobiles and with a creche placed so that the children can hold the miniature characters in their hands. Guitarists accompany the singing of carols and storytelling. The party is the thing, but the publicity—for adult consumption—is that the library party frees the parent to shop in his home town. This is an approach that endears the library to local merchants. The children seldom leave empty–handed. More often they are loaded with books.

During the school year, Saturday morning movies are presented in the library. At the end of the school year, members of the library staff visit every class in the county to talk about the summer reading program. Posters are taken to the schools and are placed at swimming pools, drugstores, and variety stores and when a staff member visits schools, she carries letters addressed to parents to be taken home by the children.

More than one thousand children join the reading club, which does tax the small staff. Our plans include small groups that meet with staff members weekly, e.g., the Stamp Club and the Nature Club. Nature clubs run the gamut of leaf identification to visits to a nearby park to study lichen and ferns. The library's June Bug Club entices young children, and the only requirement is that each child must be accompanied by a bug. At the bug club, books are spread on tables outside where identification and specimen trays relating to this project all lead the child to the use of reference material. We watch the clouds on Bug Club day. Our vivid imagination tells us the consequences of hundreds of insects, escaping from their cages and finding refuge in the building.

One summer an astronomy club met in the evening, with each child required to bring a blanket and a parent to watch the stars. The first session, held in the library, introduced sky charts, and telescopes were borrowed from people all over the area for outside use. A summer science club for students interested in depth projects meets weekly. Experiments are conducted in the conference room. (Staff members continue their duties with baited breath.)

Puppet shows always delight children, and we bring in talented people from the community to help stage them, paint props, and supply miniature furniture. A magic show arranged by a thirteen-year-old magician, blessed with talent and imagin-

Wessie Connell

ation, entranced the children. Staff members, too, had to share cushions on the floor with an overflow crowd.

Nonreaders enjoyed the "sing–along" when junior staff members held a weekly program of folk songs to spotlight the library's music collection of books and records.

Listening clubs for children, too young to read, are held once a week, with stories told under the trees if the heat is not too oppressive. The Listening Club was started many years before the Head Start programs were initiated because we found that little children at the picture book stage were envious of older brothers and sisters who belonged to organized reading groups. Special certificates are awarded these children at the end of the summer.

Summer porch parties with a Pied Piper Storyteller reach thickly populated areas. An outreach program housed in a thickly populated low–income area during the summer has featured discussion groups with films on drugs, police brutality versus fairness, and jazz sessions. A staff member tolerant of youth works with these groups.

The most exciting summer event is the annual Children's Animal Fair. A local builder of floats loans animated animals, and the library lawn looks like the entrance to Noah's ark. Passers–by stop and cars slow as the general public recognizes that a "happening" is taking place at the library. A young master of ceremonies with top hat and whip entrances adults as well as children. Brochures are tucked in children's books announcing the theme: "We went to the animal fair, the birds and the beasts were there."

Another summer event, a Doll Show, entices little girls to a tea party. Volunteers help. Special displays of dolls borrowed from doll collectors bring an older generation to the library's program, and help them to identify with youth. Brochures announcing library activities are placed in swimmer's baskets at the local swimming pool. A Turtle Hurtle is planned for some summer Saturday, with only turtle owners eligible. In the fall an annual flea market is held in conjunction with civic organizations to help the library to raise money for beautification. Individuals bring their discards and the library gets 10 percent of all proceeds.

Summertime also offers a chance for outdoor presentations of dramatic groups that use the library for practice sessions. Jazz sessions using records have brought young people into a beautifully paneled conference room. A classical guitarist entranced young adults in an indoor concert, and a philosophy professor visiting home held a roomful of students spellbound reading dialogues of Socrates. The Latin Club held an open forum with all members dressed in Roman garb.

Young people working on our staff help plan programs and if an idea is thrown out they catch the ball and run faster than older staff members. Normally seventy-five to one hundred applicants are on file for library jobs, although the pay scale is at the level of baby sitters. Community ties have been strengthened as patrons accepted the modes of dress of young staff members. As part of our public relations program we welcome staff members who exercise individuality in their life style, as it reaches their peers. This philosophy suggests that we are aware of the sense of distorted values that prompts much criticism of youth today.

A partnership, as a covenant between the library and the community, enriches both. Good public relations can strengthen both. The library is as diverse in its services as the diversity of the people in the community. Churchill wrote: "We shape our buildings; thereafter, they shape us." If the validity of the McLuhan idea, "The medium is the message," is accepted, our programs and our projects have to be relevant to the ages and stages of the individuals we serve.

Wessie Connell

5

Public Relations
for School Libraries

Ann Beebe

Ann Beebe is library consultant for Henry Z. Walck, Charles
Scribner's Sons, J. B. Lippincott, T. Y. Crowell, and other publishers. For ten years, until 1970, she was library consultant for
the public school system of Bloomfield, New Jersey. She holds
degrees from the Berkeley (Calif.) Baptist Divinity School and
the University of Washington School of Librarianship. She has
served as children's or school librarian with the Walla Walla
(Wash.) Public Library, Yakima Valley (Wash.) Regional Library,
Alameda County Library (Calif.), California School for the
Blind, Berkeley, Oakland (Calif.) Public Schools, and Monmouth
County (N.J.) Library. She has also served as Assistant Professor
of Library Science at Northern Illinois University, DeKalb, Illinois.

Quality education is the goal for which public and private schools are striving. Few school systems have managed to reach this goal for their pupils. Instead, most have managed to provide only the type of education that is relevant to today's immediate needs; this education will not necessarily help the students prepare for tomorrow's responsibilities. Better education cannot be achieved until there is better understanding by the public of what the schools are doing, why they are doing these things, and what is needed to carry out plans to meet the aims and standards of education. "Experience has demonstrated conclusively that the more thoroughly citizens understand their schools and the more they become involved in school improvement, less is the effort required for obtaining public moral and financial support which is necessary if educational progress is to be made."[1] Therefore, a good public relations program is essential to the maintenance of a good public school system.

The school library has been called "the core of the school" and "a force for excellence." These and similar phrases are widely used by school administrators, educators, and others who really understand what the library potential is in the program of the school. Yet, in many instances, the library has only a small part in the education of the children and little part in the planning and organizing of the school, its curriculum, and its program. The chief reason for this minor role played by the library and the librarian can be traced to the lack of understanding of what the school library should be doing to improve the education of the children. Thus it can be seen that a good public relations program for a school library is essential if the library is to fulfill its place in the overall educational picture.

In considering the public relations program of the school and the school library, we must first examine the place of the library within the school, although the terms "learning center," "instructional materials center," or "media center" more accurately describe today's school library. The library in this discussion is one that contains an organized body of materials for both recreational and curricular needs, consisting of non-print (films, filmstrips, records, tapes, transparencies, film loops, slides, pictures, maps, globes) as well as print materials (books, pamphlets, newspapers, and periodicals). The librarian, often called a "media specialist," is a professionally trained educator whose background enables him to work with all kinds of materials (media) in providing a program that is an integral part of the total school program.

What is the school library program? How have librarians used their knowledge and materials to aid the work of teachers and pupils? Are the resources of the school library being used to a satisfactory degree in providing creative and innovative educational programs? Such questions must be considered before a discussion of a public relations program can be undertaken, since these points are basic to the whole concept of a public relations program.

The 1969 school library standards have defined the role the school library should play in the total educational program. "Today educators and other citizens realize that educational programs of vitality, worth, and significance to students and to society depend upon excellent media services and resources in the schools."[2] The school library program provides: (a) consultant services to improve learning, instruction, and the use of media resources and facilities; (b) instruction to improve learning through the use of printed and audiovisual resources; (c) information on new educational developments; (d) new materials created and produced to suit special needs of students and teachers; (e) materials for class instruction and individual investigation and exploration; (f) efficient working areas for students, faculty, and library staff; and (g) equipment to convey the materials to students and teachers.

The most effective school library program depends upon an ongoing partnership between teachers and librarians. This is the crux of the whole matter, and is the starting point for our consideration of the total school library program. The work of the teacher is more effective and that of the librarian more satisfactory when the two plan together in providing learning experiences for the pupils. In its central position the school library offers both a resource for learning and a resource for teaching.

96   Ann Beebe

Often there is little understanding by the teachers of what the school library program is and what the library resources are for meeting the demands of creative teaching. Why have the school libraries not been used as widely as would be desired? What is the stumbling block to the partnership between teacher and librarian?

The librarian has often been lax in his planning for a total school library program that includes "public relations" with staff members. The librarian feels he can offer help, but if the offer is ignored by the teachers he must concentrate his efforts on the daily operation of the library and other successful areas of the program. He may think that some day the teachers will see that the school librarian has a particular role to play in the educational process. Perhaps he feels that teachers will assume he is criticizing their teaching techniques and methods by this offer of aid and materials, or that teachers will think he is rating their teaching as poor because he points out materials that will add to the presentation of a subject area. In these thoughts the librarian shows his own lack of understanding of the role of the school library. Before a better working relationship can be reached, the librarian himself must realize what can be done to help create an atmosphere of cooperation and helpfulness. He must be aware of what the library potential is and then make plans to carry out a program that will meet the goal of a better working relationship between teacher and librarian. He must stress the use of the library as a teaching resource.

A teacher may hesitate to ask the librarian for help because he feels the librarian is too busy to have time to work with him. He sees the busy comings and goings of individual students and classes, the constant work involved with circulation procedures, and feels that asking for help would take the librarian away from his job. It is true that any librarian can keep himself extremely busy with such everyday matters, but this covers only one phase of the proper program of the school library. The consultant role that the librarian plays in working with teachers for creative instruction is extremely important. It is up to the librarian to see that this consultant role is carried out.

School Libraries   97

Young and inexperienced teachers sometimes feel that they are showing signs of weakness or lack of preparation if they *ask* for help. They feel that they must prove to themselves, to their principals and supervisors, that they are competent to do their teaching assignments unaided. The teacher who is experienced, however, recognizes that his knowledge can always be increased and that any help which improves or enriches his teaching will be valuable. The young teachers, new to the job of teaching, are eager to accept the aid the library has to offer, if the approach is made to them by the librarian. Once they are convinced of the genuine concern for the students that the librarian shows, they turn to the library again and again, not only for aid with their class work, but also for their own college course work, their personal reading, and their own special interests. It is these young and eager teachers whom the librarian must be sure to reach at the beginning of their careers if they are to become library users.

A teacher who is about to begin a unit of study that he has taught a number of times before may feel that his previous teaching experiences with the subject have been completely satisfactory and that he therefore needs no further planning. Since no two classes of students are exactly alike, as each is composed of children with a wide range of interests, abilities, and backgrounds, each presentation of any unit of study should be planned with the particular class in mind to provide the desired individualization, inquiry, and independent learning. New materials are constantly being published and purchased for the school library. The addition of up–to–date audiovisual and print materials will sometimes make it necessary to change methods of approach or techniques of teaching, changing the process from a textbook and/or teacher–dominated teaching to a more self-directed learning that is strongly dependent upon the school library. The close cooperation between teacher and librarian is vital to this approach, and the strongest emphasis must be put on *cooperative planning.*

The librarian will provide information for the teachers about new materials and will make these new materials easily and quickly accessible. This means having a system of purchasing

Ann Beebe

materials that is flexible enough so that needed items can be added to the library when the need is there and not at some time in the future when the need has passed. A good deal of frustration has come from school purchasing regulations which require that a single, once–a–year order be placed for all materials to be added to the school library.

The librarian can be expected to help improve the learning process through the provision of materials that are created and produced to suit the special needs of teachers and students. This means the librarian must be creative in providing audiovisual and even print materials for instructional use when satisfactory materials are not readily accessible. Many teachers have found commercially prepared materials do not meet the specific needs of their classes; cooperative planning and production of tapes and transparencies seem to provide the best materials for classroom use. Other staff members may also be involved in the projects, since the librarian considers himself a part of a team and will ask for the aid of the person on the staff most likely to be able to give the desired assistance. (For example, the math teacher may be the ideal person to make charts or graphs needed to point out important facts and relationships in a social studies unit. These could then be used with an opaque projector or made into transparencies for the social studies teacher to use with an overhead projector in the classroom.) Taped interviews, poetry readings, and short stories can be used to provide just the right material at a particular time. A videotaped TV program can be used to enrich a unit and ensures that all students have the opportunity to see the program either during class time or at a special viewing. Production of such materials will be impossible in many schools because of limited facilities and funds, and the purchase of necessary equipment should be considered so that this important phase of the library program can be carried out. The writing of pamphlets, books, and plays can fill a particular need that cannot be satisfied by the book or pamphlet material in the school library. One librarian, who had some writing talent, used to adapt fairy tales for use as dramatic productions for the school radio program. She used to say with a laugh, "If we haven't got it and can't borrow it, we'll write it," in response to a request for plays for a class to perform. Others have produced books of local history or books to introduce children to the use of books and libraries which have been added to the basic curriculum materials for the school system. For example, Edna Ziebold has written two books for children on early California history;[3] Roberta Freund's *Open the Book*[4] is a guide to the program of library activities in the Newark, New Jersey, Public Schools, and this writer's own *How to Use the Library*[5] has been the text for library instruction for fifth grade students at Bloomfield, New Jersey.

The librarian provides materials for class instruction and individual investigation and exploration, materials which may be used in the classroom or in the library. A school system with a textbook for each subject in the curriculum will need additional material for the student and teacher. The textbook often gives a wide range of material but with no depth, and therefore added materials will be needed to fill in the understanding of the subject. Perhaps the textbook goes into depth in a small area only, and additional material will be used to broaden the outlook. A school system that uses no textbook at all for some subjects will, of necessity, depend upon library materials for the basic instructional materials for the subjects. A school system that uses an independent reading program instead of basal reader program must have a wide range of library books for the students to use. This might change the basic number of books that might otherwise be considered only for recreational reading in the library. Materials would have to be suited to the class to be taught with consideration of the reading levels, the range of abilities, and the backgrounds of the students.

The teacher can expect the librarian to keep him informed about any problems the students may encounter in their independent research and investigation so that the students will be given the help which they need.

Since the school library provides both a resource for teaching and a resource for learning, the librarian will be involved in the planning and the teaching of units of study along with the

Ann Beebe

classroom teacher and also in the work of the students as they seek materials and guidance in their study. The library provides students with learning experiences that are related to the school curriculum, but also with experiences created by other needs and interests. A student may seek self–improvement, better understanding of himself and his physical and emotional growth. He will find the librarian prepared to help him find the materials he needs to answer his questions and to guide him in his search for just the right amount and the right kind of information to help clarify his thinking, increase his knowledge, or broaden his understanding. He will recognize the librarian as a person of integrity to whom he can come with his request for aid in solving both large and small problems. Librarians have been quite successful in this area of their work in a school library, i.e., relationship with students.

All of these phases of the school library program are dependent upon the understanding of the role of the school library on the part of the school administration. If the school principal has little concept of the library in the modern school, the librarian has the formidable task of enlightening his administrator as to what the library potential is. Without the support of the school principal and the backing of the school administration, adequate funds will not be allocated to the library for materials, staff, and facilities. The school administrator must be a strong influence in the encouragement and initiation of innovations in curriculum planning and teaching. "In setting priorities for achieving educational objectives, he has the opportunity to press for the kind of fundamental support which a strong media program supplies to exemplary teaching and successful learning."[6]

The school board member must also have an active role in the planning and attaining of the goals for the school system. He must be aware of the educational needs of his community, and by his awareness he gives "forceful support to financial programs which may be required in order to establish excellent schools supported by the necessary media programs, staff, resources, and facilities . . ."[7]

If educational progress is to be made, public, moral, and financial support must be obtained. It is, after all, the public, or taxpayer, who provides the funds which are needed to initiate and maintain the work of the schools. The place of the school library in the total educational picture has often been overlooked or misinterpreted by the general public for whom an active school library in a modern school is an unknown quantity. Many of today's adults may not have used a school library when they were elementary school pupils, for as late as 1963 it was estimated that 66 percent of all elementary schools in the United States had no school libraries. The growth of the secondary school library was more rapid and widespread, but nevertheless the school library as a materials center is a new concept to the general public. This lack of firsthand knowledge of a school library has led to some misunderstanding or misinterpretation of the school library program. The library may be thought of as a place where a collection of books is kept, where the student may go to get a book if he wants one for recreational reading. Or it may be thought of as simply the source of the encyclopedias which the students use for information for school projects and reports. The concept of instructional materials of all kinds being readily available to the students in the school library is almost unknown to many adults. This misunderstanding or lack of information is clearly shown when requests for funds for added materials, equipment, services, staff, or quarters are met with the query, "Why do we need to expand the school library when the public library is only two blocks away?" A school principal, asking for a small sum to be used for professional reading, was questioned as to why the cost of his personal reading should be borne by the taxpayers, who obviously thought of his request as something apart from his job as administrator of the school. To many people, a school library is an extra, an educational frill, which has no real bearing upon the work of the school and which can easily be eliminated when funds are low. People often ask, "If the children want to read, why can't they go to the public library?"

Ann Beebe

Even the staff of the public library, itself an educational institution, often seems to know little about the educational processes and learning experiences. An assignment that takes students to the public library may become valueless if the staff has no concept of the purpose of the assignment. Too often a quick job of information retrieval is thought to be the best and easiest way to service the needs of students. The assignment may have been given to help the students increase their ability to use books and other materials to discover facts, to pick out the pertinent information from the material, and to draw logical and intelligent conclusions. The thinking process is cut short by provision of the "right answer" to the problem. If such work has been assigned, it should be the responsibility of the school librarian and teacher to see that the public library staff is aware of exactly how much assistance and what kind of aid should be given to the students. The school library is seen by the public library as a rival for the same patrons and the same tax dollars. But the school library and the public library each have their own separate identities and each has its own role to play. The aims and programs of each are different, and understanding and cooperation between the two institutions and their personnel are essential. The school librarian must take the lead in trying to foster this spirit of cooperation and understanding.

The foregoing discussion has shown that there is a definite lack of understanding about the place of the school library in the educational process and proves that the school and the school library must engage in a program of public relations. Because the public schools are owned and operated by the taxpayers of the state and the local community, "there is an obligation on the part of boards of education, administrative officers, and other school employees to take the public into their confidence and to provide them with the information they need in order that they understand the total educational program."[8]

What does the term "public relations" mean? Edward Bernays, the pioneer in the field, has said that public relations is the "attempt, by information, persuasion, and adjustment, to engineer public support for an activity, cause, movement, or institution."[9] It is in this context that the term is being used in this discussion. It will thus be seen that a public relations program is more than just a publicity campaign. The school and the school library must institute a carefully planned, positive program of public relations.

The American Association of School Administrators in its twenty-eighth yearbook, 1952, has listed the following purposes of the school public relations program: [10]

(1) To inform the public as to the work of the school

(2) To establish confidence in schools

(3) To rally support for proper maintenance of the educational program

(4) To develop awareness of the importance of education in a democracy

(5) To improve the partnership concept by uniting parents and teachers in meeting educational needs of the children

(6) To integrate the home, school, and community in improving the educational opportunities for all children

(7) To evaluate the offering of the school in meeting the needs of the children of the community

(8) To correct misunderstanding as to the aims and activities of the school.

A particular need exists for "the type of goodwill that results from an intelligent understanding by the citizens of the aims, the scope, the achievements, and the problems of the school system."[11] It is important that a two–way channel of communication be opened between the citizens of the community who support the schools and the professional people in the schools who conduct the educational programs.

If a public relations program is to be instituted, it must be directed toward explaining the school system's philosophy of education, aims, and means of achieving these aims (which includes the place of the school library in the total program); of interpreting the educational program to the people of the community so that it will encourage them to take pride in their schools and support them; of establishing confidence in the schools; of indicating to the public that they are receiving full value for their money spent on education; of developing an understanding of what is possible in education when adequate financial support is provided; of acquainting the public with trends in education and developments in education; of correcting misunderstandings or errors; and of helping the public feel some sense of responsibility for the quality of education of the school. [12]

These purposes can be met through a program of public relations planned to follow these steps: (a) definition of objectives; (b) definition of the public to be reached; (c) modification of objectives in light of the public so that *attainable* goals are set; (d) strategy; (e) tactics and timing; (f) culmination of tactics and evaluation of each phase of the program. [13] These steps will be discussed in greater depth so that a basis for a program may be outlined.

First, objectives must be *clearly* defined. The librarian must decide what the purpose of the public relations program is. Since the public to whom the program will be directed has little knowledge or understanding of the place of a school library in the educational system, the basic purpose must be to bring about an understanding of the vital importance of the school library in order to get support for its program. If the school librarian himself has little knowledge of modern educational techniques or is unsure of the library potential, the public relations program will be little more than a publicity campaign for some of the library's materials or activities. Bulletin boards and displays are a form of publicity that meet some needs by creating awareness and interest in an activity or materials available for the public's use. Used as a part of an overall program, they are good. These things alone, however, will not meet the need in terms of the definition of public relations we are using in this discussion. Thus, the basic ingredient with which we must begin is a consideration of our objectives.

Second, define the "public" to be reached in this program. In this case, the "public" means not the direct or indirect users of the school library (students and teachers), but also others whose goodwill and support are essential. Concern for quality education for the students must be shared by all.

Each day newspapers and magazines are full of articles about the school and the community, with reports by parents on the unsatisfactory conditions for learning in many public schools. The trend toward control of public schools in the big cities by parent groups and community groups has clearly revealed that the public had not been reached in the past with sufficient information about the schools. The parents do not know what the schools really should be doing, but they know that the needs of the school children are not being met at the present time. Yet the parents have often voted down school budgets that include money for educational improvements. Their attitude seems to be that since they didn't have such things when they were children in school, new facilities and equipment are unnecessary now. And so they refuse to pass budgets that call for newer equipment or better facilities or additional personnel.

Parents and relatives of school children, in whose direct interest a good educational program lies, are obviously an important part of our public. But equally, if not more, important are those members of the general public, the taxpayers, who have no children in the schools and thus have no direct relationship to the school system. These people, too, must be reached, for their support is important in today's battle for the tax dollar. If they see the value of a good school system in their community, a system in which a library is a vital force, backing through tax money will be forthcoming. If they have not been reached they may simply dwell on saving money.

An example of a public relations program that did not meet all segments of the public can be seen in the failure of a recent bond issue for remodeling and enlarging a senior high school in our New Jersey community. A good deal of work was done to reach the parents of school children; speakers were scheduled at each school's PTA meetings. This provided the parents of the school children with pertinent information about the need for the project, a need which would have direct bearing on the school's next evaluation by the regional accreditation team. But

Ann Beebe

little newspaper publicity appeared except to indicate that the school building was crowded. No sound reason for the enlargement and remodeling was given to the general public. When the taxpayers went to the polls to vote for the bond issue, they voted it down by more than two to one. Many of the people voting against the bond issue were those who had no children in the public school, who could not see the value to the town of a high school that would meet modern standards of space and equipment. The value of the education of the town's children was completely overlooked; the taxpayers thought only of increased taxation and not of improved education.

The public to be reached with the public relations program includes the members of similar institutions in the community, such as the public library and the museums. These institutions are the direct rivals for some of the tax money, and it is essential that their support be enlisted.

The starting point in any school library public relations campaign should be to obtain support from that part of the public with which the librarian works most directly, the teachers in the school. Backing of the school principal and the school administration (board of education and superintendent) for the school library program is also important and will make the work which the librarian hopes to do much easier.

Third, after defining the public to be reached and the goals to be set, consider whether plans are realistic. How far can the school librarian go in trying to reach his objectives in light of the current relationship between the school library and each segment of the public? Is it necessary to modify the objectives so that attainable goals may be reached? A long–range, rather than all–out, program may be necessary in order to reach some segments of the public. It may seem most important that first the teachers in the school be reached. When the results (better teaching) are demonstrated, it will be much easier to find ways to have successful contacts with other people in the public. Support for a demonstrated good is more easily acquired than for a theoretical value.

School Libraries   107

If the school system as a whole has no program for reaching the general public, it will be almost impossible for the school librarian to put on a public relations program aimed at the general public, for the school library must be shown as a valuable asset in its proper perspective as an integral part of the total educational program. The school library must not seem to be isolated from the work of the school. Therefore, the school librarian should be more concerned about reaching teachers and students within the school than uninterested taxpayers.

Fourth, the librarian must decide on strategy. How can a particular segment of the public be reached? What form will the program be? How can the teachers be reached with information that can aid them in their teaching? The strategy must take into consideration the working relationship between teacher and librarian.

What should not be done is sometimes as important as what should be done; *how* it is done is as important as whether something is done or not. An example of what should never be done can be seen in the following incident: A young and eager librarian in the children's department of a public library had decided that the local school teachers were not using the public library as much as they should for their school assignments. (She neglected to consider that an adequate school library with good professional staff was a part of each secondary school and that the town's elementary schools had good library collections supervised by two elementary librarians. She also apparently did not know that the public library had been trying to phase out the handling of classroom collections of books for the public schools since the time the elementary school libraries were organized some twelve years earlier.) She wrote a special bulletin printed on a bright, eye–catching, cherry–colored paper and sent it out to the library's total mailing list (Friends of the Library, patrons who had put their names on the list to receive library news, all schools in the area, etc.). The material on the sheet is reproduced here with only the name of the library omitted. In reading the material which came to them in the mail, the teachers were understandably angered and disturbed.

Ann Beebe

Even if every one of the statements in the bulletin had been completely true, this would not be the way to go about asking for cooperation from the public school teachers.

EXTRA

DID YOU KNOW that the library has over 32,000 books in the Children's and Young People's Departments, serving children through 8th grade?

DID YOU KNOW that teachers can borrow up to thirty books for a month to six weeks for the use of the children in their classes—and that VERY FEW teachers take advantage of this privilege?

DID YOU KNOW that a teacher who notifies the Children's and Young People's Departments in advance can have all the books on a subject put on reserve for an assignment so that the children can be sure of finding material in the library—and that NOT ONE teacher ever asks us to do this?

DID YOU KNOW that the Library will buy additional paperback copies of books on school reading lists if we are given two weeks notice of such lists—and that we are NEVER notified in time?

DID YOU KNOW that the Library staff welcomes class visits for tours and orientation—and that FEW classes come?

DID YOU KNOW that the Children's and Young People's Departments are open 54 hours a week during the the school year, including Monday evenings?

DO YOU CARE that we can serve school children much better with cooperation from their teachers?

DO YOU CARE enough to do something about it?

CAN YOU HELP by talking with teachers, bringing the subject up at Home and School or PTA meetings, etc.?

DEMONSTRATE your interest in your children!

When the indignant teachers and administrators (the school superintendent wrote a scathing letter in reply) had read the above material, they prepared for questions from parents who were on the mailing list and who might question the contents of the brochure at their next PTA meetings. The library director later wrote a letter to the teachers stating that the staff had intended no slur to the teaching staff and that all that had been wanted was to call attention to the services the public library had to offer. However, in spite of this assurance, the damage done to the working relationship between the schools and the public library has been almost irreparable.

A careful reading of the material will show that if the writer had limited her exposition to the services available and omitted the last part of each statement, which took teachers to task for their failure to make use of the services, this might have been an acceptable piece of publicity. The last four statements, the ones which urged parents to become vocal in their pressure to get teachers to make more use of the public library facilities, would not be of any value in a program such as we are trying to suggest.

The surprising thing about the whole incident was the young librarian's blithe conception that this was a good piece of public relations and that no one should have been offended by what she had written. It serves to point out that sometimes a person is so intent upon doing what he thinks is "good" that he overlooks the factor of human relations in his intensity of purpose. All public relations programs must take into consideration the public to whom the information is to go. And since one reason for having a public relations program is to change attitudes and to get acceptance for what the library has to offer, this example shows a complete lack of understanding of what should be done.

One positive thing the material in this incident did, since a copy went to each school and all PTA and Home and School

Ann Beebe

Association officers, was to make parents more aware of the services the *school* libraries had to offer. Teachers present at the meetings, who had completely adequate service for their classrooms and teaching assignments from their own school libraries, were able to assure the parents that the needs of the children were not being ignored even though the public library facilities were not used for classroom work. As had been expected, the matter was brought up at Home and School Association meetings, and school principals were called upon to make explanations to satisfy the parents.

Perhaps it should be stated that school librarians, too, often feel that teachers do not make enough use of school library facilities and materials. But the way to increase use is not by making teachers feel offended or putting them on the defensive. Thus, the strategy to be followed should be carefully planned with the human factor taken into account.

Fifth, the librarian should plan tactics and timing. Long-range plans (years) as well as short (this school year) and immediate activities should be considered.

Timing is tremendously important. A plea for more money, for example, for construction or remodeling or other costly changes, which reaches the public just at the time of a property re-evaluation will be sure to fail. At that time the taxpayer is so concerned with his probable increase in property taxes that he will feel that almost any work can be put off until a more prosperous time. The citizens without children in the public schools will not consider what the needed changes will do for the educational quality of the school system.

One very timely piece of work has just been done by the New York City schools through its United Federation of Teachers. A two-column advertisement in the Sunday *New York Times* was the first of a series to be printed under the general heading of "Where We Stand; A Weekly Column of Comment on Public Education." The column is the UFT's way of telling the public where the union stands on the important educational issues facing the city. It will be a response to newspaper editorials and an analysis of TV coverage. For "we know that we cannot improve the schools, we cannot get support for needed change without public understanding." [14]

Sixth, the librarian should carry out the tactics and then evaluate each phase of the program as it is completed.

It should be remembered that every member of the staff, not just the school librarian, has a responsibility in the program of public relations. The school principal, through his attitude and his assistance, can be the key figure. His influence will spread to all members of the school staff (including office and custodial help) to make them more receptive to the concept of the school library as an important part of the school. The teachers, through their attitudes toward the library, will help to influence the students to have proper respect for and interest in the library. The parents of the school children may never meet the school librarian in person, but they will have some idea of what he is like from their children's discussion of the library, the librarian, and the work of the library in relation to their classrooms. The students serve to interpret the school library to their parents.

It is essential that the parents of school children become involved in the work of the school; the more interest they show in the school's activities, the more support they will give to the school program. Volunteer workers can never take the place of professionally trained or regularly employed staff members, but they can be of great assistance in ways which free the professional staff from some of the non–professional duties that are a part of the operation of every school. Volunteers in the school library can provide much needed clerical help, leaving the librarian free to work with teachers and students. It is essential that all volunteers be properly indoctrinated as to what the library is trying to do and how it fits into the work of the whole school. Then the work which they perform becomes meaningful and the parent volunteers begin to have a clear picture of modern education. The chief value of the volunteers, however, may not be the actual work which they do but the influence they

Ann Beebe

exert in helping to spread the word about the value of the school library in the educational process. Often a dedicated volunteer worker becomes a powerful influence as the understanding grows as to the meaning of educational excellence. At a time when the budget may be a problem, these workers can be counted on for active support.

Not all parents can be involved with volunteer work, but many more parents than are now so occupied can become a part of the planning and guidance of the school system. This is the reason for the now widely held concept of community control of public schools. Parents are not capable of deciding what subjects should be taught and who should teach them and other such professional matters, but they can help decide what kind of schools they want and what kind of schools they are willing to pay for. The more parents become involved in the schools, the more widely spread the support for the schools will be.

In evaluating the success of the program, it is well to consider one phase at a time. Examine the results in light of what was to be accomplished. Was the goal met? Did the tactics to increase student interest in the library work? Could this be proved by the satisfied users of library materials? Did the plan to enlist teacher support for more effective planning of teaching assignments actually reach the teachers? Was even *one* teacher successfully helped?

A few questions for the librarian about his own role:

Did you find you were able to enlist principal support for your program? Did he give you backing at faculty meetings? Did he include you in planning sessions? Did he support your request for additional funds where needed for staff, materials, or facilities? If the budget could not be increased at this time, were you able to convince him of its importance so that it will not be tossed off as a frill or something expendable but will be included in the next possible request for increased funds?

Beyond the school itself, did your plan to work more cooperatively with the staff of the public library meet with success?

Did you take them into consideration in your planning, and did you keep them aware of changes in curriculum and in educational planning?

If a public relations program has been a success in any measure, then that can be the basis for additional plans for further progress in this area. If there has been little success, understanding of the reason for the failure should be used to change plans for future campaigns. Citizens know much too little about schools and modern education, and a constant public relations program must be a part of every school. The possibilities of improvement in education and the needs of the future are too little known by the citizenry of any town. There cannot be better education until there is better public understanding of the schools. Thus, quality education will not be reached until the public has a concept of a creative education that provides pupils with the skills of learning to read, to observe, to listen, to enquire, and further provides pupils with the spirit of self-motivation, self-discipline, and self-evaluation. High quality education is expensive. Educators and citizens alike must be led to see its true value in order that they will financially support programs which will provide high quality education to prepare children for the changing world of tomorrow.

Notes

1. James J. Jones, *School Public Relations*, Center for Applied Research in Education (1966), p. 1.

2. *Standards for School Media Programs*, The American Library Association (1969), p. 2.

3. Edna B. Ziebold, *California from Exploration to Statehood* (Seaside, Calif.: Perc B. Sapsis, 1969), and Edna B. Ziebold, *Indians of Early Southern California* (Seaside, Calif.: Perc B. Sapsis, 1969).

4. Roberta Bishop Freund, *Open the Book* (Metuchen, N. J.: The Scarecrow Press, 1962).

5. Ann Beebe, *How to Use the Library* (Privately published, Bloomfield, N. J.: 1965).

6. *Standards for School Media Programs,* p. 5.

7. Ibid.

8. Jones, *School Public Relations*, p. v.

114   Ann Beebe

9. Edward L. Bernays, *Engineering of Consent* (Norman: University of Oklahoma Press, 1955), p. 4.

10. American Association of School Administrators, *Public Relations for America's Schools*, The Association, 1952, p. 14.

11. Jones, *School Public Relations*, p. 5.

12. Ibid., pp. 8–9.

13. Edward L. Bernays, *Public Relations* (Norman: University of Oklahoma Press, 1952), pp. 9–10.

14. *The New York Times*, 13 December 1970, Section 4, p. 7.

6

Public Relations in a Children's Room

Marya Hunsicker

Marya Hunsicker is Consultant, Children's Services, Public Libraries Section, Public and School Library Services Bureau, State Library, Trenton, New Jersey. She holds a B.A. from McGill University and a master's in library science from the University of Michigan. Her past jobs have included work as school librarian in a new school, reference librarian, supervisor of an evening branch library, and summer playground bookmobile librarian in Los Angeles. She was also director for three years of the Swarthmore (Pa.) Public Library and served a short stint as Children's Librarian of the Northport (N. Y.) Public Library. For five years she taught English and children's literature at a Japanese university, has recorded almost a hundred hours of English language folktales for use in teaching English to Japanese, and has discussed—in Japanese—children's literature on Japanese television.

The old story tells of six blind men who were introduced to their first elephant. One, who felt the animal's tail, marveled at how like a rope an elephant is; another felt the giant animal's knee and argued that the elephant was really like a tree, and a third, feeling the smooth sharp tusk, declared that "Tis mighty clear this wonder of an elephant is very like a spear!"

One evening I asked a group of children's librarians each to describe what she felt was the most important feature of the public relations program in the children's rooms of their libraries. Their responses ran the gamut from: "Plenty of films; that really packs them in" to "A friendly attitude" to "Well, we don't have to advertise; we're busy enough with those who are coming in now." They were, in fact, a huge conglomeration of tusks and tails, of ropes and trees—for, like an elephant, a public relations program *is* a colossus, a huge super–structure far easier comprehended by the part than the whole.

My own feeling is that the single essential feature of any successful public relations program is that it must be an integral part of the entire library program. Good public relations do, and should, begin with a good library program. Writing news releases, constructing posters and displays, and giving talks—these are all part of a P. R. program in its most overt sense. Few of us, however, would wish to use these and the other techniques of publicity to disguise a poor library program; we use them instead to advertise a good one.

And, what's more, a truly vital library program will generate much of its own good public relations. It will do so by word–of–mouth and it will do so because really good and full library service is an exciting and a frequently newsworthy happening. The public library that specializes in having a variety of live animals in constant residence in its basement children's room—including, one summer afternoon, a baby elephant—doesn't have to fight for newspaper space; the reporters come to them. And so do the kids. This concept of good service being the first stage of good public relations seems to fit well with the definition of public relations formulated by *Fortune* magazine some years ago as "good performance, publicly appreciated because adequately communicated."

This is an excellent definition of what we're talking about; it's also a discouragingly broad one, encompassing everything, all the activities that go on in our children's room—from keeping the floor swept to running a summer reading club to defending *Sylvester* before the Policemen's Benevolent Association. What I would like to do in this paper is to concentrate on only two aspects of this broad spectrum of services that are particularly fundamental to good performance and, by extension, to good public relations. I see these two very broad practices actually as two precepts of library service:

1. Meet people and meet them well.
2. Keep the library alive, varied, and sensitive.

We all know that these two principles, important as they are, are by no means the whole story of good library service. I see them rather as the tusk and the tail, the beginning and also the end of good library service and, thus, of good public relations in the library. They are particularly important because, unlike other aspects of library service, they represent goals and principles for not only the children's librarian and the professional staff but, instead, they are achievable concerns for all who work in the library. Let's look at each carefully and in some detail.

First, the tusks—and, let us honestly admit that many of us at least some of the time really do bare our tusks at our public. We've been short with them on the phone at the end of a long day; we've taken a youngster to task for bringing a book back late; and haven't we all too often fallen back on that most egregious tusk–baring greeting of all: "Did you look it up in the card catalog?"

These things may not happen often or even happen in every library, but happen they do—and they represent not only poor library service but worse public relations. Meeting our public well begins with meeting each of them personally as he comes into the library. I believe that every child has the right to be greeted with a smile when he comes into his library. As one librarian put it, "Even a wave will do," but some form of

Marya Hunsicker

greeting is essential if we are to take even the first step toward meeting our children well. That same librarian recalled the store her father owned when she was growing up. He had painted a bright line across the floor; anyone who could get across that line without being greeted would have a 10 percent reduction in his bill. Couldn't our children's room use such a friendly line? Couldn't we all stand a reminder that a friendly welcome to everyone who comes through our doors is one of our first and our most pleasurable duties?

Meeting our patrons well, furthermore, involves positive action on both sides of the line of greeting. Once a child is in the library, he has the right to be treated with the same courtesy and consideration that an adult patron would meet. He has the right to be able to speak aloud, not merely whisper; to walk, not tiptoe. He has the right to expect to be served, not taken through a series of lessons on everything from "how to use the library" to the moral values of returning one's books on time.

The idea of being there to serve our public is fundamental to the idea of meeting them. Pleasant and willing service is not generally a common experience today, but the public library is one institution that has always tried to give more than lip service to the concept. Our professional courses in general library service, in reference, in children's work all speak again and again to this point. Professional literature repeatedly emphasizes the concept of service. Professional meetings frequently deal with such service-oriented subjects as "the reference question," and "handling the complaint,"—all of which emphasize our professional concern and awareness about the rights of our patrons. Presumably, the professional librarian knows and understands this responsibility well.

But what about the clerk behind the desk, the library worker who never went to library school and who never has the opportunity to go to professional meetings, yet who is very likely the first and the last person in the library the child meets? In selecting our clerical help, do we particularly look for people who have this special ability and desire to "meet people and meet them well?" What kind of in-service training do we give them that emphasizes not merely the routines of their work but the philosophy of service that lies behind those routines? Why, if we feel professional meetings and associations are still important in keeping the professional staff informed and up-to-date in their work, do we make no place in our state Library Associations for our clerical workers? Surely they have as great a need as do professional librarians in upgrading their library skills and philosophies.

Our children's librarian has put together a particularly successful training program for the clerks employed in her section. She says, first and foremost, in hiring she looks for a friendly attitude. This is far more vital than any specific skills or predetermined educational background. This is the quality that her library program is built on. One of the invaluable suggestions this librarian gives in her training program is that the desk clerks make full use of the name on the child's card; they learn to call the kids by name, letting them know that they personally are welcome and a part of their library. The final step in this training program is the most delightful innovation of all. After her clerks are thoroughly trained in the skills of their jobs and indoctrinated with the service concept that is foremost in that children's room, they are then frequently and willingly loaned out as one-day replacements in the adult section of the library. This librarian reports a far more positive attitude toward children throughout the entire library staff as a result of this practice.

The obligation to meet people does not end with greeting the children who actually come to the library. Most of the children in our community do *not*, in fact, use their public libraries regularly and, if we are going to meet them, we are going to have to get out of our libraries to do it. We need to visit Scout troups, Junior Audubon Society meetings, and 4-H groups. We need to go to the places and meet the other people who are working with children—the many specialized agencies, such as the Easter Seal Society and the Association for Mentally Retarded Children, juvenile detention homes, community recreation centers, and the Park Commission. We should not only be meeting the other professionals who work with our children but should be serving

Marya Hunsicker

along with them in the regular week–to–week activities of parent–teacher organizations, on the Girl Scout council, the Head Start board, and even the English curriculum committee at the high school. All these things are possible; all are desirable if we are to be able to offer the best in library service and the widest possible public relations program.

Above all, we need constant close contact with the schools. Fortunately, many of our communities today have well–developed school library facilities and the public library is no longer expected to take on either the job of supplying all the school reading needs or that of instructing the children in the use of the library. But school remains a place where most of our patrons are most of the time, and there are plenty of areas in which these two major educational agencies, the public library and the public school, can still cooperate. The first thing to do in establishing a working relationship with the local schools is certainly to talk with the superintendent, the principals of the various schools, and their school librarians. Ask for an opportunity to attend one of their staff meetings or possibly their pre–school year orientation sessions; invite the school librarians to hold one of their meetings at the public library; suggest to the teachers your interest in visiting their classes, possibly with a story on a subject they are currently studying; bring the seventh and eighth graders booklists and book talks full of the kind of books *they* want to read. And then, when classes visit the public library, scrap the time–honored lessons on how to use the catalog for the rare adventure of a told story.

In all instances, I feel contacts with adult groups are better made with a specific purpose in mind, with a definite idea of something you could do for them or, frequently equally useful, something they can do for you. You might, for example, use the local Council on Drug Abuse to work with you on a bibliography on drugs to be distributed in your community; contact the special education department of the schools asking if they will work with you in establishing a summer story–time especially for handicapped youngsters; ask the schools that are planning to be closed during the summer to lend you multiple copies of twenty to thirty sure–fire titles that are on a reading list you will be featuring during the summer. Or do as several New Jersey libraries have recently done and see if the local American Association of University Women will put together and maintain small experimental "science in a shoebox" kits for circulation in the public library. One New Jersey library uses the public school's Art Department regularly to provide monthly displays for the children's room—mobiles, paper–mache masks, clay statues, and all kinds of drawings and paintings. This library even goes one step further and gives each child whose work is displayed a note to take home:

> *Susan Brown's* art work has been selected for display at the Bergenfield Public Library during the month of *March*. We hope you and your friends will take this occasion to visit the library and to enjoy the display.

And they do come, often people who would never otherwise come near the library. Once again the library has shown that by extending their services to meeting and working with others outside the library, they have effected good public relations.

This particular practice also fits the second of the criteria listed earlier for good library service—the need to keep our libraries alive, varied, and sensitive. The wealth of colorful art, prepared by the children and hung by the school Art Department, keeps the library bright and alive and thoroughly attuned to the kids themselves. Surely if we wish to keep our libraries sensitive to the needs and desires of our children, we need to have the children involved in the library itself. Such an art program is one way. This sort of patron involvement can also be done by tapping the youngsters' eagerness to help, their eagerness to be part of the institution and not merely served by it. A group of junior volunteers can readily be formed in most communities to assist with such jobs as pulling cards from the catalog, pasting pockets, pulling ratty old books off the shelves for replacement consideration, and even helping at the juvenile charging desk. Such a work brigade may go only a little way toward lessening the librarian's work load, but it ought to go far in keeping the lines

Marya Hunsicker

of communication open between the library staff and the kids they serve.

It is possible even for the kids to very actively participate in and contribute to that most "professional" of activities, materials selection. Janet Burness, Children's Librarian of the Bergenfield Public Library in Bergenfield, New Jersey, has long had a program which gives her young patrons, particularly fifth and sixth graders, an opportunity to express how they would like things done in their library. Her Junior Roundtable Discussion Group, which meets once a week during the winter months, has been asked at various times to read and evaluate for ordering purposes the periodicals collection in the children's room; to look over and react to a pile of picture books left for reviewing by one of the library vendors; to choose between several different recordings of *Peter and the Wolf* the library was contemplating purchasing. Mrs. Burness says of her program that the kids' evaluations are generally infallible. If a book was weak, they could spot that weakness immediately. They were among the early ones in the cheering section for books like *Where the Wild Things Are*, a title that some librarians were slow to pick up. The kids brought to their selection job a far wider variety of tastes and interests than could ever be represented on any but the largest of library staffs; it was, in fact, the tastes and interests of the library reading public. And, as a side effect they definitely took away from these meetings an increased ability to read critically and to understand better the library's job. Again, the quantity of "selection" the kids accomplished was negligible, barely a drop compared to the amount of work we expect from our children's librarians. The growth and understanding on both the children's and the children's librarian's part was the important thing.

We have always tried, however, by one means or another, to have a collection that is full of variety. Increasingly, our libraries are trying to see that the types of materials in our collections display a similarly wide scope. In addition to books and periodicals, a large number of children's rooms also have picture collections, pamphlet files, phonograph records, and at least some access to films. A few stock games and toys, framed art reproductions, and even pets for circulation. Perhaps the biggest single boost that has recently been given to the development of our materials collection is the growth of the cassette business. When you send a cassette out with a library patron, be he young or be he old, he is, in fact, a veritable walking advertisement for the library and its services. His parents, taking their nine–year-old on a two–week auto tour of the Western states, will love you for keeping him occupied during the day with recently taped versions of the Newbery books. Passers–by on the street will readjust their pace in order to keep in step and hear the end of some Egyptian folktale he's listening to on cassettes. In crowded elevators, on the school bus, on the beach and the ski slopes—within a matter of only a year or so, cassette players are going to be everywhere and the public library should prepare to be part of that movement. That's part of our job of keeping the library and its collection alive, varied, and sensitive to what the kids want.

Another increasingly used means of bringing immediacy and variety to the total library program is an increased use of library-sponsored programs. Almost all libraries have always had some kind of programming for their children. Most universal, of course, have been the story–orientated programs—either pre-school programs or formal story hours for older children. Increasingly, however, libraries have injected new life and new variety into their schedule of library programs. During the past year in New Jersey, I have heard about kite flying programs, a talking bird show, a series of lecture–demonstrations on the use of cosmetics, puppet shows, embroidery classes, a cooking class in the library, a karate demonstration, and a hobby swap–shop held in various children's rooms. None of these programs revolved around stories or even particularly emphasized books. All were immensely popular with the youngsters in their communities. In talking recently with a group of children's librarians who are particularly active with programming in their various libraries, I heard over and over again the librarians confirming the fact that generally the most successful sort of programs in their

Marya Hunsicker

libraries are those which actually involve the children at some point. The same concept was expressed a different way at a recent New Jersey State Library–sponsored workshop on young adult services, a meeting that brought some thirty teens and approximately seventy-five library directors and their young adult specialists together. The idea was expressed again and again that the youngsters ought to be formally involved in the planning of all library activities. There ought to be a Teen Program Committee, with the teens themselves the principal members; the kids should be represented on a Materials Selection Committee; and even, as is the case with at least one New Jersey library, be a member of the Board of Trustees of the library. This idea of assuring teenage patrons an active voice in the planning activities of their libraries came up so many times and in so many forms in the course of the workshop that one might almost think it was a really new concept, a revolutionary one.

It's no such thing, of course. What it is, is just good common sense. More than one library has watched its entire eight-week schedule of once–a–week evening films for teens flop dismally when the library failed to schedule the programs on the night that the kids had said was best. Getting the kids involved in the library's programming is also both good library service and good public relations. Furthermore, it can begin, to some degree, as young as the third grade. Some libraries allow the children to actually do programs in the library—produce their own puppet shows; run their own in–library coffee house; at the very least, help pick out the stories for the next week's story time.

Even if the children cannot contribute too much in the planning stages, the programs can be arranged to let them take some part in them. An animal show in which the kids can hold various wild animals; origami demonstrations with the audience making at least a few figures themselves; sing–alongs—these participatory types of programs are almost guaranteed successes.

Programs that simply involve children, even if not local children, also tend to meet with success. One library met with wild acclaim when the library took up the wax from the floor of its children's room and invited in a championship junior roller skating troup for a demonstration. My nine–year–old Oriental daughter and I have done some very happy programs in which we reenact a typical child's day in Japan, beginning with Jennie stretched out on a Japanese bed mat, through an actual breakfast of raw egg and seaweed, to my telling a Japanese folktale. Still another proven success in programming occurred when a dog trainer, his young son, and their prizewinning German shepherd demonstrated their techniques. One feature that all these successful programs had in common, apart from their use of children in the actual programs themselves, was that none were "talk shows." They were programs with a good deal of action and demonstrations, programs that used slides and films and songs—and this is as it should be. An active schedule of programs should exemplify the great variety of information and of pleasure that are in the very nature of all our libraries. They also will illustrate the tremendous variety of media that is increasingly being made available through our libraries. Programs, viewed in such a light, fit well with the second demand that our libraries be places which are alive, bright, and sensitive.

Nor should the library's programs be restricted to the library building. Almost every trip outside the children's room results in new contacts, new variety and scope to the total library picture. An out–reach program can be something as simple as a deposit collection, large or small, paperback or not, placed in a hospital, in doctors' and dentists' waiting rooms, and above all at the community swimming pool. They could be in terms of a small book display on flowers and gardening placed in the local florist's window; on cars and racing in a neighborhood Pontiac franchise display case; on any of a myriad of subjects represented by the library collection placed as mini–exhibits in any of many small businesses with public windows. Best of all, out–reach can be in terms of real programs—services extended outside the library walls. Non–library story hours have been especially popular—stories told in parks and day camps, at special schools and detention homes, at Scout meetings and private parties, on street corners. Last summer one intrepid librarian decorated the sides, front, and rear of the family car with huge

Marya Hunsicker

figures of the seven dwarfs—and, of course, the name of her library—and drove through town, ringing a bell, and calling kids to sidewalk story–times. It was a tremendously rich offering in neighborhoods that generally had but small contacts with libraries. It, like most such out–of–library activities, was also good public relations and attracted newspaper and radio attention throughout the area.

As I've talked about various aspects of public relations in a children's room, one thing I have hardly mentioned is publicity. Quite the contrary, I have put a lot of stock in word–of–mouth, in the ability of a good service and a good program to attract its own attention. I do, however, believe very ardently in publicity, in all the standard and most obvious ways of getting the library's program, both its specific day–to–day activities and its broader aims and philosophy, across. I am a strong supporter of news releases (and, please, not just lists of new books); of posters and displays both within and without the library; of talks before all the various civic groups that will have you; and of school fliers. I think the library story is an exciting one and one well worth the telling.

So many channels for telling that story are open to us. We all, of course, already know about and make good use of the newspapers to announce coming programs, rejoice over past triumphs, and to provide occasional human interest items. Are we also utilizing the very considerable number of special newsletters and house organs that circulate in all of our communities? If we have taken an earlier suggestion to heart and gone out to meet the people who are active in various specialized associations, then we will already know about the YWCA's *Public Affairs Council Bulletin*, or Frontiers in Adoption's quarterly *Newsletter*, or any of the other scores of similar organizational organs available and eager to receive news items of potential interest to their specialized readers. In addition, a number of children's departments also already issue their own monthly newsletters or news fliers, distributed across circulation desks or through the schools.

Another potential source of advertising for library activities in a number of communities is the community calendar, a listing of goings-on within the local area. Such calendars are sometimes produced by the Jaycees, the Chamber of Commerce, or the Recreation Commission—but, in the happiest of instances, by the public library. Huntington Public Library in New York State is one library that has undertaken this community service, and has found it to be an activity that gets the library's name and activities monthly in large type into a heavy percentage of homes in that community. Although initiating such a project would probably not be within the scope of the children's room alone, it is certainly a service the children's room should encourage and contribute to heavily.

And then there are the many opportunities to speak to groups and organizations in the community, not merely to talk about what the children's room does but to show them. How about a demonstration pre-school program for the Lions, Kiwanis, and Rotary Clubs; a sample story-time or book talk for the PTA and at church suppers? Remember, these adults may not be our patrons, but they are very definitely the parents of our patrons and, as well, the taxpayers that support the library's activities.

I have heard children's librarians declaim that they don't need any more publicity; they can't handle the crowds they are already getting. The problem here, of course, is that if a library is filled to bursting with 200 kids for a film and 100 more turned away, that library needs two showings. If there are waiting lists for the four pre-school programs already scheduled, that library needs to schedule four more—and advertise them in the community for *all* the parents to know about, not just for those few who happen to see the small notice at the circulation desk or who happen to share a coffee klatch with another mother whose six-year-old attended last year.

Of course, it's entirely possible that your harassed children's librarian just can't fit in another session—then, all the more reason for more publicity, eventually to justify appropriations for additional personnel. Library publicity is not aimed only at our

Marya Hunsicker

young patrons to keep them informed of what we are doing; it must always also be directed at the entire community that supports the library to keep them informed of what we might yet do. Most of us need more personnel and we need better funding for the greater variety of materials that today's public should expect to find in their libraries. To gain these things we need to keep the library and its activities ever before the community and, particularly, before the decision makers of the community. Good programs and good services will keep the public coming to us; good publicity will insure that those who control the libraries' financial support will be informed of those good programs and services.

And this, I feel, brings us back to where we started. The fact is that all libraries and all children's rooms have "public relations." Whether those relationships are good ones or not depends first and foremost on whether the entire library program is sound or not. And the soundest library program is one that will keep good public relations as a primary goal of all that it does.

7

Selling the Academic Library

Eli M. Oboler

Eli M. Oboler has been Librarian of Idaho State University and its predecessor, Idaho State College, Pocatello, since 1963. A graduate of the University of Chicago, he received his library science degree at Columbia University, and was on the staff of the Chicago Public Library and the University of Chicago library before going to Idaho. He has been a lecturer in the Great Books program at the University of Chicago, and is the Bibliographic Consultant to the Great Books Foundation. He is editor of the study, *College and University Accreditation Standards*, has served as editor of *The Idaho Librarian*, and has been on the Board of Editors of *College and Research Libraries*. He is now completing a book on libraries and censorship.

The old traditions of the college student as a captive audience for his institution's library is outdated. In these days of political activism, multi-media interests, and overcrowded campuses the library must do a real selling job, or fall behind in the competition for campus attention. The reserve book room or desk may have its involuntary devotees, but the use of the rest of the library is more or less dependent on the quality and quantity of the public relations practiced by the library.[1]

The library? That is a *building* and its contents. Rather, by the *staff*—professional, clerical, and student. Each of these groups has an appropriate part to play in helping convince the library patron that he or she must make the library a regular place to visit and use. And all of the members of the library staff must do all they can to establish a favorable image of the library by what they *do*, rather than by what the words issued officially from the library *say* they do.

It is of little use to keep talking—in the school's catalog or the library handbook—about the library as the heart of the college or university if this is not more than an empty phrase. When an academic library is really attuned to its institution and its patrons, and the library staff is made up of trained, devoted people who really help, rather than individuals who concentrate on shushing noisy students and requiring minute observance of finicky rules, public relations are easy. All that a library staff person charged with the specific, official public relations responsibility (and every academic library should have someone so designated) has to do, in the smoothly functioning institution, is to "tell it like it is."

No academic library ever has enough funds or enough staff or enough reading materials or—except perhaps during the first year after a new building or addition is opened—enough space. But every academic library has excellences and services, achievements and timely events, of which even regular library habitues may not be aware. There is no portion of the academic community that has more of general interest to tell and, unfortunately, that usually tells less. And then usually the library tells that little badly.

Basically, the academic library has three audiences—the campus, the general public, and other libraries. The modern academic library, if it is doing its job, should be producing publications and information of value far beyond its walls. Surely, particularly in tax–supported institutions, the tax–paying constituency and the legislature are both entitled to know what the library is doing beyond the routine level. And in private colleges the alumni is an analogous group, concerned and curious.

Let's be more specific. First, what groups actually on the campus are—or should be—interested in the library? The administration needs to know whenever the library produces a worthwhile bibliography, or prepares an absorbing exhibit or display, or obtains a useful new library–related machine, or performs an unusual service, or receives a gift of some consequence. The faculty and staff—and especially immediately involved departments or services—should be informed of these happenings also, preferably through whatever medium is commonly seen by the faculty and staff. The campus newspaper, an obvious public relations target for the library, should have either a regular library column written by a library staff member, or a reporter should be assigned to the library as his regular beat, if the editor can be so persuaded.

Incidentally, like all other library news releases, whatever is sent out to the campus paper should avoid the didactic and the dull. Perhaps that is not so incidental, either. Today's public is not going to read a dry book review of, say, *The Tergiversations of Antimonianism* or a similar specialized work. Either write a timely, absorbing comment, calculated to be of wide interest, on one or more books, or an appropriate, readable description of a lesser–known library service—or forget it. Save the expository material, dull or not, for handout library manuals or leaflets. These also should be as interestingly written as possible, geared to attract the reader and not likely to be thrown away.

Academic libraries, no matter how many millions are spent on staff and books or palatial buildings, must work toward good public relations with their regular patrons. They must

Eli M. Oboler

have useful direction signs and understandable card catalog instructions. As has been said, "Eschew esoteric and sesquipedalian verbiage," or more simply, say what you have to say and what needs to be said, then stop.

But don't count on prior knowledge of how to use a library, whether by students or faculty. In particular, most librarians seem to think that it is not asking too much to expect high school and college graduates to understand the difference between the Dewey Decimal System and the Library of Congress Classification. This is important knowledge to have because many academic libraries are reclassifying. It should not be taken for granted, however, that most patrons understand how to find books in a library with two classification systems. This may appear to most academic librarians as very obvious stuff, but experience in many academic libraries seems to justify bringing public relations down to a very simple level indeed.

Along with the ABC's of public relations go, of course, more advanced ways of telling the library's story. For instance, in every library there are particular excellences. Why not, along with other matters, feature these as part of the regular series of library displays? It is sometimes hard even for the library staff, especially in a large library, to be aware of the wide variety of special collections in the library system. Don't hide that manuscript collection of the writings of a popular author born locally, nor neglect to tell about the complete set of a relatively uncommon reference work that should be made known to all.

Prepare your displays on a planned, coordinated basis. Keep in mind that one closed book looks much like another when set up on display. Use the full panoply of display and exhibit materials that even modest academic libraries have available—pegboards, exhibit cases, bulletin boards, plastic letters. Other devices and tools are procurable in a wide range of complexity and price.

For over a decade the Idaho State University Library at Pocatello has been presenting a regular series of book and other reading–material displays calculated to interest its campus community in reading matter that it might not otherwise discover.

Selling the Academic Library   137

The topics have included current materials; annually recurring celebrations of such events as United Nations Week, National Library Week, Brotherhood Week, and Christmas; and, what has seemed of most interest, celebrations of various anniversaries connected with outstanding individuals and events.

For example, in 1957–58 there were displays commemorating both the Alexander Hamilton bicentennial and the William Blake bicentennial. In 1958–59 there was the celebration of the Theodore Roosevelt Centennial and the sesquicentennial of the birth of Abraham Lincoln. In 1959–60 John Dewey's 100th anniversary and Daniel Defoe's 300th anniversary were both commemorated. In 1960–61 the 150th anniversary of the birth of Leo Tolstoi, the 200th anniversary of David Hume's birth, and the 100th anniversary of the beginning of the Civil War were among the displays included. In 1961–62 the library featured the sesquicentennial of the birth of Charles Dickens and the 200th anniversary of the birth of William Cobbett. For 1962–63 Idaho's Territorial Centennial and the fourteenth year of independence of Israel were celebrated in displays.

In 1963–64 there was, of course, the 400th anniversary of William Shakespeare's birth. In addition, a continuation of the Civil War Centennial was featured. The 50th anniversary of World War I was the feature of 1964–65, as well as the 100th anniversary of the birth of Henri Toulouse-Lautrec. The bicentennial of the birth of Thomas Malthus was featured in 1965–66, and in 1967–68 there was the 50th anniversary of the beginning of Soviet Russia. The fact that it was 300 years since the death of Rembrandt was celebrated in 1968–69, and 1969–70 was highlighted by the 100th anniversary of the birth of Mahatma Gandhi.[2]

An infinite number of possibilities for thematic displays can be found, once a display program is decided upon, but in general displays at Pocatello were of four types: those featuring an anniversary; celebrations of particular "weeks"; displays on particular topics of general interest about which materials could not be found by looking in one place in the card catalog; and displays concerning specific library services. As the years went

Eli M. Oboler

by, some displays were concerned with controversial and currently relevant themes.

A listing of the main and subsidiary library displays in the ISU Library for 1969–70 may be useful:

Tomorrow's Careers
Mahatma Gandhi (100th Anniversary)
Western Books
United Nations Week
That's a No–No! Drugs, Liquor, Marijuana and Tobacco
The Defense of America: ABM, CBW, etc.
The Arts in Flux: Art, Drama, Music, Film Television
Happy Holidays
The End of the Empires
A Feast of Short Stories
The British Museum and Its Publications
Prehistoric Fauna and Flora
Brazil: A World in Itself
The Draft
America the Un–Beautiful: Why Conservation?
The United States Supreme Court: Center of Controversy
The American University Today

Humanities

Christ and Revolution
Thar's Gold in Them Thar Stacks
Books from Down Under
America's Black Writers
Fiction of the 60s
World of Art
Religion in Turmoil

Science

The World Population Explosion
The Sea: Its Poetry and Practicality
Gems, the Uncommon Stones
Sweeteners; the Bitter Pill

Social Science and Documents

The Blacks in American History
Law Enforcement
Japan in the World Picture
United States Wildlife
India, Feeble Giant
Brotherhood
The Far East
New Life for American Cities
The American West
The American Campus
Help for Small Business
Air Today and Gone Tomorrow
The Challenge of Crime
Come Josephine (aviation)
100 Years of the Weather Bureau

Other Display Topics

Smithsonian Institute and the Arts
United Nations Week
Today's Isms
Communism: Theory and Practice
Christmas in Other Lands
Winter Sports Scene in Idaho
Poverty in the United States
American Foreign Policy: Are We Over–Committed?
Latin America
United States vs. Environmental Degradation
History of American Labor Unions
Blacks in American Politics
Learn All the Rules of Your Favorite Summer Sports
Nixon's Brain Trust

The technique used in preparing for the display, once a subject was chosen, was simple and direct. To begin with, the library card catalog was consulted for appropriate subjects and

Eli M. Oboler

cross–references. Second, the current *Books in Print* was consulted for the particular subject, and the books that seemed suitable and not already in the library were selected. If appropriate, government document sources, the pamphlet file, and periodical indexes were also consulted, as well as specialized bibliographies on the specific topics.

Meanwhile, original posters dealing with the various topics were drawn by a student staff worker so that they would be ready at the time of the displays, which were normally planned to continue from two to three weeks each, during the following school year. Announcements of the displays were sent out ahead of time to the local newspaper and to the student campus newspaper, as well as to the weekly campus calendar. A continuing space on the main student bulletin board in the Student Union was used to publicize each current display, under the heading "The ISU Library Presents."

Not all the displays attracted an equal amount of attention, but it was evident, from requests that were made at the time and later, that many of the materials on display were new to the campus reading community. The reading list series—now numbering over fifty—of the ISU Library are based mainly on displays.

The displays are varied in format in several ways. Pegboards, as the locus of each display, are used to exhibit pamphlets, documents, and clippings, not just books. Appropriate magazine and newspaper articles and photographs are clipped from duplicate materials throughout the months before the scheduled dates of each display. Then they are reviewed for timeliness, appropriateness, readability, and appearance. Sometimes one table is used, sometimes two; sometimes one three–section pegboard, sometimes two; occasionally both sides of each panel— variety is the mode for attracting maximum attention.

Ordinarily all items on display are available immediately for circulation. The ideal display is one with about fifty items originally, all of which circulate before the display period is finished. Incidentally, attractive book jackets are always kept on file for possible use in displays.

The beneficial results of the ISU continuing series of displays are so evident that other academic libraries might well consider at least a modified plan for continuing displays. They decorate the library; they attract readers. They result in the satisfaction of the main drive of any librarian—getting the right books and the right readers together.

Another quite popular means of accomplishing two goals of academic library public relations is through the "Friends of the Library" group. With growing financial pressures on academic administrators, the possibility of new sources for new library funds is always welcome. And library "Friends" groups, which can be organized in a myriad of ways and for many different purposes, are proving to be a rather easy means of getting both friends of the library and more funds or materials for the library.

Perhaps the zenith in American "Friends" groups is the one at Brandeis University, which for many years, through various schemes for raising money, has provided practically all the regular book purchase support for the library there. But this is an unusual, probably unique, situation, not likely to be a national model. Still, it indicates just how far such a group can go if it is dedicated.

More commonly, "Friends" organizations, usually composed of alumni, strive to bring in collections or individual books that the library needs but is unlikely to get through normal funding channels. Some academic libraries have found "Friends" groups less effective than direct pleas to the alumni through the regularly published alumni news. At Idaho State University the direct approach has proved quite successful, with the help of effective cooperation from the alumni director, library staff members, and interested faculty.

If an academic library does sponsor "Friends of the Library," it should not do so in a token way. Time for planning, provision for at least annual meetings, and some preliminary expenditure of funds for literature with which to contact potential members and for mailing costs are essential.

Eli M. Oboler

Another important public relations device for the academic library is its correspondence. If forms and letters sent out from the library give the impression that the library conforms to the stereotype in which a horn–rimmed, dour–visage spinster sits waiting for the unwary patron to violate a piddling rule, the library cannot expect to be popular. Many libraries that spend much time and money on internal displays, signs, and publications send out forms and letters that should be obviously recognizable as counter–productive.

No one expects an academic library to run without reasonable rules involving such matters as the circulation of books, the hours of opening, interlibrary loans, overdue charges, and so on. But what faculty member or student is not likely to cut to a minimum his use of a library that sends curt, jargon–filled notices? Granted that with the vast student bodies that some major libraries must accommodate, it is difficult to keep the human touch. Yet such a simple step as revising forms and letters to sound less formal and impersonal would help most academic libraries, of whatever size.

Letters from the library to prospective employees are important too. Most academic libraries are always engaged in recruiting potentially valuable new staff members, and it is disheartening to see how careless many letters of this type are. (Just as this is being written, the academic library administrator in a nearby county seems to be dealing with a buyer's market, where there are many more qualified applicants than there are openings. Naturally, this has not always been the case, nor is it likely to continue to be so.) But no matter what the state of the library employment market, every applicant, whether his application has been solicited by advertisement or otherwise, or even if it is sent in unsolicited, certainly deserves the courtesy of a personal, not a form letter, one which is without question in reply to his. Each of his specific inquiries should be answered, and he should be sent as much information about the library, the institution, and the community as he seems to deserve in terms of his potential for the specific position or for employment at *any* time in the future. One never knows when failure to reply personally to a letter may eventually result in bad public relations for the library. But this should not be the motivating factor for what are, after all, the fundamental ingredients of all public relations, simple courtesy and good manners.

The real test of public relations, in the long run, is service. All the elaborately printed and flossily decorated booklists and handbooks, all the news releases, all the displays and signs—these and other more visible examples of dealing with the library's public cannot compare in importance to the way the library staff behaves toward patrons. It is ridiculous when an academic institution spends ten million dollars on its library building, a million dollars on furnishings and machines, and vast continuing sums on staff and reading material, only to have all these made naught by a two dollar an hour student assistant who behaves contemptuously or carelessly to the patron in the library.

It is well worth any academic library administrator's time to be almost as careful in the selection and retention of student and clerical assistance as of professional staff members. The library that willingly accepts the leftover students seeking employment in the university, those students who are neither intellectually nor emotionally suitable for library work, deserves the bad public relations which will almost inevitably result. And in-service training, rather than chance assignment of tasks, is the key to a cooperative, well-trained student assistant.

A student library assistant's position should not result in special library privileges. If a book, for example, is on a two-hour reserve, it should not go out for three hours or more to an individual who happens to be on the library staff. The head of the library, too, should observe meticulously every rule that he expects others to observe, or fairness and equity really do not exist in the institution he heads. Surely public relations will suffer, once special privilege becomes known, as it always seems to. This applies even to the treatment of such august individuals as deans and bursars and vice-presidents and even presidents and board members. They may grumble when forced to comply with the rules, but they will appreciate the honest endeavor of

Eli M. Oboler

the library staff to give everyone an equal opportunity to use the library's resources.

One aspect of academic library public relations that deserves particular mention in these days of "participatory democracy" is the image the library staff presents in its dealings away from the library with students, faculty, and administrative staff. The library staff that becomes ingrown and omphaloskepsistic will not know what its patrons really think about the library and its services, and may take actions contrary to widely expressed needs.

Too often it is the head librarian alone who is known as an active participant in the broader affairs of the institution, and all too often this is the fault of the head librarian. He should encourage active participation in faculty affairs, even including what may be considered to be routine committee meetings. This plea for active participation does presuppose that the professional librarians on any academic library staff are full faculty members—but that is another story! Nonetheless, the professional staff that accepts as a continuing obligation its share in faculty life is much more likely to be accepted as full colleagues by other members of the faculty than the staff that isolates itself.

On sprawling campuses with long distances between the main or branch libraries and such general faculty meeting places as dining rooms and cafeterias, it is a great temptation to librarians to meet and talk with other librarians only. But more good will can be engendered in a ten–minute conversation over coffee than can possibly come out of reams of mimeographed, canned publicity.

At the very least, an occasional note or phone call to a faculty member, on a matter that may be of particular interest to him, can be rewarding. There is no need to pester these busy men and women, but there is every need to help them by reminding them of the particular book that has just arrived in their special field, or by asking for information only their expertise can provide, or in other ways indicating that the library is not simply a collection of closed books. Even auditing or taking an occasional class for credit is an aspect of making the library staff visible, a segment of a good public relations program.

As has been said earlier in another connection, probably the most important single concept in formulating an academic library's public relations program is service. The librarian who forgets that the library is auxiliary to the major function of his institution will not bring books and people together, and any library can lapse into weakened repute if it is not providing timely, efficient, and useful service.

For this reason, the library public relations program, although preferably coordinated by a single individual, should be part of every library department's plan and program. In the small library, it should be handled by the library's head; in the medium–sized library by an assistant or associate librarian; in the large library, by a trained public relations professional. It should be an active part of every day's operations, whether in reference or circulation or interlibrary loan or acquisitions or cataloging. It can work only if each member of the library staff on every level is constantly doing his share.

The library public relations program is usually divided into three portions: publicity, public relations, and publication. No amount of any one of these will make up for a reasonable presentation of the others, so they all deserve attention.

If the parent institution's news bureau is flooded with reports of trivial library "news," it is unlikely that releases will ever evoke more than "My God, more library stuff!" as a reaction from the news staff. Judicious selection of news of relevance, likely to be of interest to the entire campus community and preferably also to the outside community, will result in the publicity the academic library needs.

As a rule of thumb, if the campus newspaper prints an average of one item a week and the local newspaper one a month, the library is probably getting its fair share of publicity. Not all stories need to be written up in detail by the library's own reporter. If the material to be released has elements of wide interest, call the news bureau and/or the campus paper, ask a

146   Eli M. Oboler

reporter to come over to see for himself, and if appropriate, ask a photographer to come along to take pictures of the display or the new book purchase. It is of importance to the whole campus if your library, for example, is computerizing its circulation procedures or its catalog; it is certainly big news if your hours or fine rules are being changed. Remember, undue modesty never will result in due publicity.

Internal public relations are most significant to the success of the library, but they are likely to be given short shrift. Ask any academic library administrator what he is doing for good public relations among the staff, and he will probably wonder what on earth you are talking about. Yet one can walk into almost any academic library, unfortunately, and without prying find unmistakable evidence of alienation between departments in the same building or on the same floor, not to speak of branches outside the main building. One notes damaging lack of information about what is going on outside of each little bailiwick. One hears too often that "they" are making the decisions, and that "no one ever tells us what's going on."

What should be the most common and important single regular publication of any academic library with at least five staff members is a regularly issued—preferably monthly—staff bulletin. It can be an invaluable adjunct to library public relations.

It need not be as elaborate as some of those that have reached the size and consequence of being indexed in *Library Literature*. It does need to be an honest and thorough report of what is going on in the library, ranging in topics from plans for a new library building, remodeling, or annex down to a fair representation of the achievements of each department within a particular month. There is really no need to report, for example, that the leggy blonde student library assistant at the reserve desk is engaged again—but a wedding date, even among students, certainly deserves mention. The addition of a new typewriter to the catalog department's holdings hardly matters, but plans for use of a commercial or cooperative cataloging service affects the entire library, and should be reported.

Selling the Academic Library   147

Include in the bulletin library and social news. Usually two or three pages per month will suffice to keep the staff informed, unified, and loyal. Send a copy of the staff bulletin each month to the news bureau and the individual to whom the head librarian reports. Every member of the library staff, including the newest student library assistant, should be on the distribution list for the library staff bulletin.

Other publications that should be included among the modern academic library's public relations tools are reading lists, handbooks (student, faculty–graduate, or general), library–use aids (customarily one or two–page leaflets), and bibliographies of particularly significant holdings in special fields. The reading lists and bibliographies normally should be publicized in statewide, regional, and national library media, so that others may be informed of their availability.

More than any other type of library, the academic library tends to get into a rut. Academic library administrators often feel that their captive audience will use their library without inducement or advertisement. Such administrators permit the public relations of their library to become at best a series of routine announcements—cursorily prepared, desultorily issued. Then, when the library really needs its public—when the budget declines, or when the "new" annex has become old and further building is required, when the library initiates a drive for faculty status, rank, and salaries for a staff that had not achieved these essentials—it discovers that it does not have its backing.

It is obvious that the best public relations any institution can have is good performance. That performance would be even better if a professionally planned and executed combination of publicity, public relations, and publications let all the various publics of the academic library know just what the library is really doing. If the staff knows that its accomplishments are widely reported, it is much more likely to do a good job.

The academic library today is far too complex and costly, and far too significant for the education of its student patrons and the research and teaching needs of its faculty, to permit its

Eli M. Oboler

use to languish. The image of the academic library can be good or bad, accurate or false, depending on its public relations.

If fewer students or faculty are using your academic library, don't fool yourself by saying "They just aren't reading any more" or "Today's students get their reading out of the bookstores" or "The faculty here is just too busy to come in." Let your patrons—actual and prospective—know what your library has to offer—and then get out of the way of the rush!

Notes

1. This article was first presented, in somewhat modified form, in the *Idaho Librarian* (October 1970), pp. 135-138, under the title "Displays for the Academic Library."

2. Good sources for ascertaining such anniversaries, whether of people or events, are the following:

Black, A., and Black, C. *Writers and Artists Year Book*. Boston, The Writer; Annual.

Mirkin, Stanford M. *What Happened When*. New York: Washburn, 1966.

Chases' Calendar of Annual Events. Flint, Mich.: Apple Tree Press, Annual.

Williams, Neville. *Chronology of the Modern World*. New York: McKay, 1968.

DeFord, Miriam A. *Who Was When?* 2nd edition. New York: Wilson, 1950.

8

Public Relations and the State Library

C. Edwin Dowlin

C. Edwin Dowlin is the State Librarian of New Mexico. He was formerly head of the Development Division of the American Library Association, Head Cataloger, and Assistant State Librarian of Ohio. He holds a bachelor's degree from the University of Colorado and a master's in library science from the University of Denver.

Times have changed for the State Library. For decades the State Library got along rather nicely by doing what the name implies—giving library services. Rural residents may have received their books in collection boxes, or from a bookmobile. State officials may have enjoyed special reference privileges, but on the whole the State Library operated as a large public library. State Libraries have had a much grander role in mind, for a long time. But the truth of the matter is that development efforts were not as fruitful as desired, and the support generated was not a major factor in State Library survival. It is no wonder that State Libraries were not prepared for the turn of events in the 1960s.

Libraries of all types actually began to move toward the formation of regional and statewide systems after decades of talking about cooperation. The formation of systems across "type of library" lines required a go–between, and the State Library was in the logical position to assume this role. The inclusion of funds to promote interlibrary cooperation in the Library Services and Construction Act found a great many State Libraries unprepared. Individual libraries already involved in film circuits, forming consortiums, and cooperating in processing center organization were much readier to take advantage of sound leadership before most State Libraries were prepared to give it. Quite a few State Libraries had not fully adjusted to this situation by 1970 when the *Standards for Library Functions at the State Level* made this role official.

This newest role for the State Library is primarily administrative. The services performed have fewer direct and immediate benefits to a taxpayer. Unfortunately, the same sequence of events that brought about the new "leadership" role also brought a general taxpayer's revolt. The State Library is faced with competing for the tax dollar with welfare, health, public safety, and formal education to meet a responsibility for organizing and financing statewide systems. The provision of materials and allowances for their organization are given low priority in planning "action programs" to solve human problems. To meet the challenge it has been given, the State Library must develop much stronger support for its efforts than has been possible in the past. A strong public relations program is obviously needed.

State Libraries have always recognized their dependency on public relations. The failure to develop strong general support through public relations is due to a number of factors that hamper efforts to develop the total public relations package for State Libraries. The problems cannot be dismissed as lack of preparation on the part of the State Library.

What's Holding Up the State Library?

Every library is influenced by its placement in a legal body, and the State Library is no exception. Administrative patterns established for all agencies within the framework of a state government apply to most State Libraries. Salaries and fringe benefits are part of an overall structure, and the State Library is likely to be a low priority. Purchasing requirements, inventory controls, and personnel recruitment involve miles of red tape. In the few exceptional states, the State Library may be highly susceptible to changes in the political winds.

The public still tends to equate public relations with sales campaigns or lobbying. Taxpayers have not accepted the view of economists who see government as a productive activity— recognizing that better understanding of the nature of government operations and services can be beneficial. Although the use of the term "public information" has helped, the function is still considered something of a luxury. It is unlikely that substantial funds will be made available in the foreseeable future to hire a professional public relations expert for the State Library.

Federal funds have created some situations that will haunt State Libraries in the future. The Federal library legislation that provided a financial bonanza for State Library programs also designated the recipients of the services. The old Library Services Act supported a rapid expansion into the countryside. But the State Libraries that chose (or felt forced by circumstances) to operate this extension program raised a specter of competition in the eyes of librarians in smaller towns.

C. Edwin Dowlin

Each new State Library service meant another group of supporting customers. The institutionalized and the handicapped received new books; communities with matching funds were given new buildings. So long as the funds kept growing, the State Library was a hero. All of these programs involve permanent personnel, equipment, and group claims on future costs.

As the program matured, hints of future problems developed. New York State found that its services to the handicapped were limited by the Federal program. The State was reluctant to fund a program where Federal funds were available, and the Federal funds were insufficient to meet the demand for services. The Library Construction Amendments of 1970 have added more categories eligible to receive funding, but the outlook for increases in Federal funds is dim. The State Library is likely to be the goat in the struggle brewing over allocation of available Federal funds among the groups of its clients. Unless these pressures can be focused on Congress and state legislatures as funding sources, frustration will result for all concerned. The major urban libraries that saw little need to participate in earlier distributions, are now toying with the idea of direct allocations from USOE as an answer to the crises they face.

State members of the profession tend to view State Library attempts to strengthen its position with some distrust. Large budgets, a mobile staff, and a central position in communications are strengths upon which to build a public relations framework. Precisely because they recognize these strengths, librarians question how they will be used. Requests for greater authority to enforce policies and regulations can give rise to suspicions, which have some basis in fact.

A few State Librarians have a little game they play. The State Librarian or his deputy sees a problem, decides upon a course of action, then calls in those involved for advice. The participants in the game must guess the course of action already decided upon and ratify it. For some reason, players of the game sometimes become somewhat cynical.

Professional lack of interest can be overcome, as Sally Farrell has shown in Louisiana. By outlining the problems, specifying the practical limits of the situation, and agreeing to carry out the solutions, the Louisiana State Library leads the state into an enviable period of steady growth of systems. Meanwhile back at the ranch, there has been considerable agitation to remove the Federal requirement for advisory councils. These councils give advice that some State Libraries don't want.

A sound public relations program must be based on truth, and the way others see that truth. Every action and word must reinforce the central truth or "theme" to be projected. Anything else seems to bring out an unnatural selfishness, fierce independence of spirit, and general lack of respect for the State Library. Projecting truth is much more difficult for a large agency whose theme is administrative in nature, in which the projects and activities are numerous and frequently uncoordinated. Where others must be consistent, the State Library requires "congruency." The term is borrowed from Karl Rogers, the father of nondirective counseling. The concept requires that every utterance, every action reveals both the overt and hidden meanings as one. Somewhere short of undiplomatic bluntness, an audience must know exactly where the State Library stands. When combined with respect for other professionals, congruency provides a solid base for building a public relations framework. Application of the concept of congruency contains implication for staff training, program development, and the approach to communications.

Denouncing the historical constraints won't solve the problems, but it is useful to know the tasks faced. Several State Libraries are looking for positive approaches to building program support. The most likely solution appears to be that of total approach to the problems of developing leadership roles. Clues seem to be lying about in pieces. The best illustration comes from an analysis of personal experience in the Ohio BOOKS/ JOBS program.

C. Edwin Dowlin

BOOKS/JOBS and the State Library of Ohio

BOOKS/JOBS was one of those flashes that never reached its full potential because of the lack of follow-through. The clarity of hindsight made it an extremely valuable learning experience. The need to relate individual projects to overall long-range State Library objectives was the greatest lesson to be learned. The project suggested that decisions to allocate resources, the involvement of all the staff, and the overall "image" of the State Library were basic to success of an individual project. Furthermore, the general overall climate of the State Library will determine whether a project will add to or subtract from the attainment of long-range objectives. It was my conclusion that, regardless of whether a public relations consultant was involved, the responsibility for development of a long-range strategy for communications is inextricably mingled with overall administration. BOOKS/JOBS also suggested that the chief administrator of the agency could develop this strategy as an alternative to hiring the specialist to provide necessary planning continuity. A total review of the operation with an eye to developing the basics of a communication pattern is the necessary first step. A new approach to carrying out the role of statewide leadership is needed. Some specifics of the BOOKS/JOBS project show this.

On Shaping a Message

It is widely recognized that a club is needed to get a mule's attention. However, people take exception to being assaulted, no matter how delicately, unless a strong message related to *their* interests follows. This message should be simple and strong. BOOKS/JOBS had such a message. "Libraries go into action on a social problem," would be the headline. Unfortunately, many readers missed the fine print which limited the scope of the part that libraries would play in this effort. The idea that libraries would help people find jobs was intriguing. It was also inaccurate. The project was designed to place libraries in the position of coordinating community efforts to provide useful information to job–seekers. BOOKS/JOBS also provided library materials to those who were in a position to work with job seekers. Despite the drawbacks, the BOOKS/JOBS message showed the value of a message relating to united action in applying information to human problems. A few of the librarians were shocked at this way of looking at their services; many more were delighted. For the many librarians who were disappointed in the lack of followup provided by the State Library, the BOOKS/JOBS project was an object lesson in the value of having adequate State Library staffing.

The BOOKS/JOBS message had the advantage of bypassing one of the dilemmas of the dual message that State Libraries must project. In its coordinating role for all libraries, the State Library can play an important part in uniting local library messages to interpret the role of the library in our society. This interpretation is critical, but it is equally important that the public understand the unique contributions that administration plays in a statewide library program. BOOKS/JOBS sidestepped the problem by showing the State Library as the key element in local developments.

The BOOKS/JOBS message made news, as a foot–high stack of newspaper clippings attests. It showed that people can relate to an action program more readily than to the grand goal of developing library services for all. State Libraries have the opportunity to relate their messages to the human development priorities of the state. The major difference of this approach is in an orientation to audiences rather than capabilities.

Audiences for the State Library Message

Choices of audiences for public relations are practically unlimited. BOOKS/JOBS had two primary audiences: librarians and those who needed information to work with the unemployed and underemployed. The general public was a secondary, but more responsive audience. The only available analysis of the classic audiences for the State Library is found in *The Library Functions of the State.*

C. Edwin Dowlin

This study suggests seven possible audience categories for the State Library. These categories are dependent upon:

1. the quality of service given to state government
2. the prestige of the State Library as an intellectual institution
3. the services given directly to borrowers
4. the interest in extension and development programs
5. the support of influential organizations
6. the support of the organized education profession
7. the personal influence of the agency head and staff

These categories are rather vague and overlapping, but they are the ones available at the moment. An equal effort in each category will not yield equal results, and success in one area will have a positive effect on closely related areas. The first four of the categories seem to be those most closely related, and these are the areas where the more successful State Libraries have excelled.

Experiences in several states indicate that the support of state officials who are pleased with the service they get from the State Library can be a pivotal factor in obtaining funds for other services. Over a long period of time, many agencies and legislatures have developed their own libraries because their needs were not met by the State Library. Where this has happened, the cards are stacked against the State Library wishing to expand its official clientele. Staff and material will be lacking to carry out a broadened program where little or none existed before. Agencies that have developed their own information services tend to see a newcomer as a competitor for state funds. It is not wise to ask alert government officials to pay for duplicate resources. When agencies and legislatures have not yet recognized the demand for information services, they are not likely to be easily convinced by public statements of the need.

The results are worth fighting for, despite the handicaps. As a statewide network resource, the State Library can specialize in governmental information and use Federal funds for materials and personnel. By working closely with newer agencies, the State Library can offer samples of its service in the form of current awareness projects. Many officials who are short of funds are delighted to learn that the State Library has, or will obtain, materials they can use. Furthermore, departmental libraries are often quite narrow in the materials they contain. The departmental librarians may welcome consultant and backup services. Opportunities to explain information services as part of regular training programs should be sought out; and if no training exists, then the library may even cosponsor them to get them started. Although serious barriers do exist, several states are demonstrating that they can be overcome. The eventual goal is for state officials to discover the benefits of a centralized service even though the need for specialized departmental libraries continues to exist. The entire effort is a facet of the public relations program, of course. Ohio successfully invited the participants of high–level management training programs to have a dinner in the State Library. A short tour and a brief explanation of State Library information services were coupled with the offer to enroll in a rudimentary current awareness program. Most participants were delighted to discover the services available.

I venture to state that too much reliance has been placed on support by borrowers who receive direct service from the State Library—especially in the case of the rural user. This support is easiest to obtain and shows up as a strong pressure group at the Federal level. It is useful, but somewhat less effective at the state level. The missing element in working with the state legislature appears to be the strong, independent legislative effort of the type supplied by the ALA office in Washington.

Attempts to organize statewide friends groups have never been very successful. The persons who would be natural members are usually deeply involved in local efforts. Logic dictates that an alternate form of organization be devised, but it remains to be done. The use of advisory committees has been a help, but efforts in this direction have never been successfully integrated into ongoing tasks having state–level significance, as opposed to Federally funded programs.

C. Edwin Dowlin

It is reasonable to expect continued emphasis on statewide library extension and development, and the support of state professionals will be crucial in these efforts. Professional support is precarious at best. With the resolution of a crisis or the passage of major legislation, the busy professional librarian must return home to face the tasks that accumulated while his attention was distracted. The support of the profession is most difficult to achieve and maintain in areas with large concentrations of librarians and complex organizations. The only hope is to work to incorporate statewide planning as a continuous process into the schedules of the professionals. Ohio has had some success in doing this with annual planning conferences sponsored by the State Library and the Ohio Library Association. The principles of working with "emergent groups" apply in developing broad-based state participation in planning. Advisory committees, conferences, and the work of the professional association are vital. While P. R. is one important factor, such things as timing, philosophy, and leadership are more elemental to success.

Techniques of gaining the support of influential statewide organizations require applying local success stories to the state scene. The success in cultivation of partisan political support is much more important at the state level, however. Suggestions that State Libraries seek to be involved directly in the political process have this support in mind. Because of the strings often attached, the individuals may find their usefulness waxing and waning. These efforts are typically fronted by Boards and Commissions that serve as "bumpers."

Deliberate efforts to enhance the prestige of the State Library as an intellectual institution are dangerous. Social climbers and ambitious bureaucrats do this. On the other hand, when the State Library performs capably, and an audience understands this, the message gets through. Thus, the most deliberate effort should be to select and train highly qualified staff rather than to communicate directly.

At one time, local educators—the community teachers or principals—were the primary support group for public libraries. Because the State Library was helpful to these public libraries, and a substitute where school libraries did not exist, strong support came from this audience. In general, the activities involved teaching the kiddies reading skills and giving them the reading habit.

Times have changed. School libraries are developing rapidly and are taking over a major portion of this task. On the state level, the loan of children's collections and related efforts are largely vestigial remnants of bygone days. In the same way, small towns have been brought into the center of the latest fashions and modes by the automobile and that great civilizer, television. The decline in influence of the literary club of *Main Street* reflects a lessening of the mystique of reading as an "in" activity. People are reading more than ever, but as required to carry out their tasks of daily living. State Library efforts to hark back to the good old days when the public library ranked with elementary education as a community priority are doomed. A quick check on the percent of educational funds spent for public libraries and the State Library will show how serious this matter has become.

BOOKS/JOBS received considerable support from educators although it was not child oriented. A Cincinnati guidance counsellor made an impassioned plea to librarians to include his well-to-do suburban library branch in the project. He needed the materials in his work with high school students. A community action worker saw the need for a project in the territory he covered. He visited and was turned down by three local public libraries before he convinced the Board president in a fourth of the need for participation.

The State Library staff itself should be added to the obvious audiences. Staff members not directly involved in a project are an important communications channel. They create a climate that encourages understanding and enthusiasm.

The Need for Communications

The BOOKS/JOBS project had a great many problems. Chief among these were the shortages of State Library staff members

162   C. Edwin Dowlin

to follow through with the necessary activities of answering questions, providing assistance, and organizing training sessions to help the libraries capitalize on their situations. The lack of one or two individuals coordinating these efforts and the flow of information prevented the BOOKS/JOBS project from realizing more than a fraction of its potential.

BOOKS/JOBS serves to illustrate the possibilities for overcoming the barriers to developing a framework for public relations programs in State Libraries. It is not being proposed as a solution to these problems. Most State Libraries have already shown themselves capable of having a brochure designed, or a news release written. Although these can be valuable aspects of a public relations campaign, their effectiveness will remain limited until communications strategies are developed as inherent in State Library decision making.

9

A Newspaper Library's Public Relations

John Rothman

John Rothman is Director of the Library and Information Services Division, *The New York Times.* He was for many years
editor of *The New York Times Index.* He holds a bachelor's degree from Queens College, New York, a master's from New York
University, and a doctorate in comparative literature from Columbia University. He has lectured at the Pratt Institute, at
seminars on information retrieval of the American Management
Association, and serves as consultant to the American Association of University Presses.

It may be well to state at the outset that this chapter is based largely on my experiences at *The New York Times*. To the extent that *The Times* is atypical, some of my information, observations, and conclusions may not be equally applicable to other newspapers. In discussing mutual problems with librarians and information specialists of other publications and related institutions over many years I have learned, however, that the library operations of *The Times* differ from those of other publications not so much in kind as in degree—in the range and scope of the information processed, and in the number of inquiries and quantity of materials handled.

"Library operations" is not really an accurate term; what we are concerned with might better be called "information facilities." At *The Times*, the information facilities consist of the following:
- the archival file of *The Times* itself, issue by issue (once this was maintained in bound volumes; now it is on microfilm)
- the clipping library, or "morgue"
- *The New York Times Index*
- a Reference Library
- a Photo Library
- a map and chart section
- the Information Bureau, which handles a limited range of mail and telephone inquiries from outsiders (discontinued December 1970)
- a Research Section, a small group of professional researchers working directly with the news and editorial staff

In addition, there are numerous ready–reference shelves and special–subject collections (for example, Sports, Gardening, Food and Restaurant News) maintained by and for the use of individuals or specialized departments.

Fundamentally, we have here what any publication must have in some degree: a collection of all the items that have appeared within the publication itself and a variety of other items —books, periodicals, pamphlets and so on—that are used as background and reference materials, all organized and processed in some way for convenient storage and retrieval.

In any publication, such collections are originally organized and maintained for the use of the staff. Archival copies must be maintained for legal and business purposes, to help in processing complaints, and to provide reporters and editors with what has already been published on a given topic. Photographs, maps, and charts are collected so that a variety of appropriate illustrations may be available whenever editorial matter requires. Material from other sources is collected to provide background data and possibly divergent views and interpretations. Reference works are acquired to assure the accuracy of published material, and to enrich the contents of the publication.

Yet the publication's usefulness to outsiders is not at all limited to the current, the latest, issue. (We learned long ago that yesterday's newspaper is by no means dead.) Readers want to consult back files of a publication to look up details on a given event, to check on a name or a place, to compare a situation now with a similar situation then, to reread a feature article. Most publishers furnish back files in some form to satisfy this demand, and thereby serve not only their readership but also their own economic interests, for the use of a publication for reference purposes tends to increase its standing and prestige, and thereby its circulation (and, also, the supply of back copies may be revenue–producing).

The basic public relations task for newspapers, then, is to furnish back issues, or information from back issues, to inquirers in convenient form at minimal cost.

This sounds very simple, but there is a whole host of problems connected with it.

Back issues have to be stored, and this requires space and personnel. Then, how many copies do you produce for archival purposes? How do you store the copies so that they remain in order and in good condition? *The Times*, for many years, produced bound volumes of fine ragpaper copies; but these became prohibitively expensive, too difficult to store, and too heavy to handle. Now we produce microfilm; but this, too, has its price,

John Rothman

and it is sometimes cumbersome to handle and difficult to read at length; and separate machinery is required to make copies from it (and these, too, have their price). So, gradually, a complicated program has been evolved that offers back copies of the paper itself for limited periods in limited quantities, as well as microfilm at reasonable cost and diverse copying services.

Frequently the inquirer wants more than just to get hold of a back issue—he wants a specific item, and he doesn't know in which issue he might find it. He suspects (often he darn well knows) that the newspaper has the back files organized in such a way that its personnel can locate specific items easily, be it through a classified clipping "morgue" or through some kind of indexing or cataloguing scheme, and he wants to take advantage of this facility. Why should he conduct a laborious search himself, when someone at the paper can probably get him what he wants much more quickly and easily? He is rarely aware that such a request may be an imposition and that the multiplicity of such requests may constitute an intolerable burden for the publication. The hapless librarian or information assistant handling these requests often becomes his accomplice: for one thing, he does not wish to offend the inquirer; for another, it is often easier and quicker to get the answer than to explain why he should not be required to get it.

Long ago, *The Times* decided to make its Index available to the public, as a handy device for searching the file of back issues for specific items. For many years this was a public service run by *The Times* at a substantial loss, and there were times when its continuance was in serious doubt. Few publications have a back–file market large enough to permit them to create similar indexes; and although the inquiring public (as represented by public and other libraries) has repeatedly signified its desire for more such indexing services, it has so far not signified any willingness to support them financially. In consequence, published indexes are provided only by organizations able to justify them economically or to absorb the cost; and elsewhere the inquirers do their searching without an index, or try other sources—or call the newspaper librarian.

At *The Times*, we have run into a further complication. Some inquirers may not have ready access to *The Times Index*, or may run into difficulties using it, and get the idea that their search of the *Index* might be conducted much more efficiently by someone with ready access to it and thorough acquaintance with it. And who is more likely to have ready access to and thorough acquaintance with *The Times Index* than a staff member? Hence our *Index* staff is faced with an additional number of inquiries for material from the *Index*, and, again, they often answer these, partly to avoid giving offense, and partly because a refusal would require more time and effort.

The prize possession among a newspaper's information facilities is usually its "morgue," in which clippings of published materials are stored in separate folders by subjects, names, places, and organizations. For the public, this is the ideal facility for consulting the paper's back files—not only is everything on a single topic together in a single place, but it is in the same form in which it was originally published. It is the actual article clipped from the publication, not some surrogate. And this, of course, is the one facility that is usually barred to the public altogether.

The reason for this prohibition lies in the nature of the material. Clippings tear easily and get yellow and brittle quickly; the more they are handled the shorter–lived they are bound to be, and thus access to them must be kept to a minimum. Furthermore, it is impossible to keep the clippings in the desired order. In a morgue of any appreciable size and value, a staff of attendants is employed to furnish clipping folders to users and to return these to their proper place after use; this staff would have to be increased drastically if the morgue were to be opened to the public. Finally, the files often include material from other publications and reporters' notes and other unpublished material, and this could not be made available to outsiders for obvious reasons. The knowledge that such material is included often is the major element in an outsider's request for special permission to use *The Times'* morgue; and the lengths to which some of the more persistent people will go to get this permission

John Rothman

—the extraordinary alibis, the complicated ruses they think up—
are amusing as well as amazing.

(It is because of our awareness of the value our morgue has
as an information resource that *The Times* has undertaken its
Information Bank project, a pioneering system by which our
morgue materials are being processed into a fully automated
computer facility that can be used by the public.)

Our Photo Library's relation with the public is beset by
similar problems, on a smaller scale. Prints of *New York Times*
photos are available to outsiders at low cost, but the burden of
finding the picture in the files of the newspaper, so that a copy
may be ordered by date and page of publication, falls on the
purchaser. We can neither search our files of some two million
prints for him, nor let him do this search himself; the first is pre-
cluded by the lack of personnel, the second by the lack of space
and the nature of the material. (Files of photographs, like files
of clippings, diminish in size and deteriorate in quality in direct
proportion to the number of times they are used.)

The photo files, of course, include far more than prints of
Times pictures. There are pictures taken by our photographers
but not published (often a whole film, thirty-six exposures, is
used for one event, but only one shot may be published), and
there is a vast quantity of wire service, studio, and publicity pictures. Obviously, *The Times* can make available to the public
only its own pictures. This is another reason why use of the
Photo Library is restricted to the staff.

Back to the principal body of material, the published text
of the newspaper, and another major problem: what to do about
material published only in earlier editions or in subsidiary,
regional editions of the newspaper.

Most newspapers publishing more than one edition designate
only one as archival. Newspapers that distribute different editions to different areas, varying the content on a geographic
basis, usually make the "central city" edition or the one with
the largest circulation the edition of record. When, as in the
case of *The Times*, the differences between editions is chiefly

A Newspaper Library   171 one of timing, it is usually the final edition that is used for archival purposes.

Preserving, storing, filming, and indexing a newspaper is costly enough when there is only one edition; if the process is applied to several editions, the cost increases dramatically and often becomes prohibitive. Either the several editions must be processed in toto, in which case much material is handled redundantly; or they have to be compared carefully to one another so that only unduplicated material will be processed, and the cost of this in time and manpower would be enormous. Obviously, the need is greater where material varies regionally than where the difference is chiefly between earlier and later versions of the same story, and my understanding is that most newspapers publishing regional editions make the effort to preserve all significant material and make it accessible in some form.

The Times endeavors to preserve all early–edition material that does not find its way, in some form, into the final edition (the only one that is microfilmed and indexed), but the procedures to collect such material are not completely reliable, and alternative procedures that would give us complete reliability are economically prohibitive. The material that is collected is stored in the morgue and made available to the staff only. Inevitably, readers wishing to retrieve items they have read in an earlier edition find, from time to time, that some of these did not get into the final edition and hence cannot be located through the *Index* and on microfilm. Inevitably, complaints about this give rise to proposals that we index and microfilm such material as well. As I said, the high cost makes this impossible; but there is also an important policy consideration: the final edition represents the ultimate that the talents and judgment of *The Times* produce each day, and therefore quite properly the only one to become the edition "of record"; the earlier editions are in a sense interim products which are completely superseded by the succeeding edition.

Again, it is usually the newspaper librarian or information assistant who must field the readers' complaints on this score, and—as you will surely agree—the explanation is complicated

John Rothman

and perhaps not ever wholly satisfactory. And, again, the publisher must find a happy—or, if not happy, at least a tolerable—compromise between the amount of help and information that the public wants and the amount he can afford to provide.

Let me turn from the material resources to the human resources of the newspaper's information facilities and their relationship with the public. No matter how large or how small a newspaper's library–information staff may be, one of its functions is to answer inquiries from the public, whether they are made by mail, by telephone, or in person. Such inquiries, of course, do not always go to the librarian or information assistant directly and many do not get routed to him at all, but are received and processed by business departments, executive offices, and especially the news and editorial departments—and there most frequently by the desks or individuals assigned to special subject areas, like sports or food news. These, then, become willy–nilly a part of the newspaper's library and information function and carry out a substantial portion of its public relations. (I am not including here the syndicated columnists responsible for letters, columns of advice on health, child rearing, marital bliss, wise shopping and the like. I have no direct experience with this kind of operation, but I believe that these columnists maintain their own "library" and have their own information assistants and run their own public relations, quite apart from the newspaper in which their columns appear.)

It is curious to note that the inroads that radio and television have made on the newspaper business have apparently not affected the newspapers' library functions at all. The latest bulletins may be had instantaneously on the airwaves—but people still call or write to their local newspapers for information, and in ever–increasing numbers.

Although *The Times Index* and *The Times* on microfilm are on the reference shelves of many libraries, and even though *The Times* itself maintains a street–floor office in midtown New York where these may be consulted (with an information specialist in attendance), the flood of telephone calls to our Information Bureau during its last few years exceeded a quarter million a year, and the number of letters has averaged three hundred a week. (And this does not include the number of calls and letters going to other departments, as noted above.) The information sought ranged from references of published material, to statistical data, to some item that will settle a dispute or decide a bet; to advice (we usually refused to give any), to identification of people or places; and around Easter and Christmas we regularly got requests from students, more or less disguised, for help in writing term papers.

We recognized long ago that the huge volume makes it impossible to render satisfactory service to all callers, and before we discontinued this service in December, 1970, we had to restrict the scope of the Bureau's operation so that we would not, by rendering extensive assistance to a few callers, preclude many from getting any service at all. Even so, we were sure that many letter writers resented the check–marked form reply and many callers were frustrated by the "sorry, but . . ." they got instead of the desired information. We hope that the technology of the future will enable us to substitute a satisfactory self-service system for at least a major part of this operation.

A newspaper's store of information is not limited to what is published in its pages, or even to what is stored in its files. Beyond this is the information accumulated by its reportorial and editorial personnel as a part of their total professional experience, and this, especially in regard to the specialists, is a resource of tremendous value for the newspaper as well as the public. The reputation of a newspaper hinges to a considerable extent on the number and the reputation of authoritative people who write for it on specific subjects. These people, then, have their own direct relationship with the public, in that they get voluminous mail and telephone calls, are invited to address meetings and participate in panel discussions, are asked to contribute to other publications, write books or have some of their writings reprinted in book form, and so forth. These activities sustain and expand their fame (and often bring them substantial additional revenue), and this in turn benefits the newspaper that employs

John Rothman

them; the public, on the other hand, benefits by having access to some of the top experts in their fields.

And yet, this relationship has its problems also. A sensible balance must be struck between how much time and effort the expert should devote to accommodating the public, and how much he can spare; and a sensible balance must be struck between how much help the expert needs and how much the publisher can afford to provide. The expert has his own sources of information, which he stores in his office for ready access; he normally builds his own file of clippings of his work as well. He usually gets some staff assistance in maintaining this collection, and usually these aides help in answering calls and in sorting and answering mail. Multiply this by twenty—the specialized departments of a newspaper (art, food, gardening, home repair, music, stamps, travel and so forth) easily add up to twenty—and you have a sizable effort and expenditure for this area of public relations. We have no statistics on all this at *The Times* except for one department: some time ago our Sports Department tallied the number of telephone inquiries it received in a certain period, and came up with the staggering annual rate of over 65,000! Most of these calls, incidentally, were from fans who wanted historical data, not current scores or schedules.

All of this is indeed a function of a newspaper's information facilities, but it would be unwise to try to have the library or information staff take it over. For one thing, the librarian would have to search out the answers to many questions that the expert or his aide would have at his fingertips; for another, the direct contact between the public and the expert is an important factor in good public relations that should not be abandoned or reduced.

At the beginning of this chapter I said, "The basic public relations task for newspaper libraries is to furnish back issues, or information from back issues, to inquirers in convenient form at minimal cost." In the light of all the preceding discussion it may be well to broaden this statement considerably.

The basic public relations task for newspaper libraries involves far more than the library itself, far more people than the librarian and his staff, far more than the back issues of the paper. The task is to make the aggregate knowledge and information encompassed by the newspaper's current and past issues, its background and reference collections, and its personnel available to the public, conveniently and economically. The task further is to do this in such a way that the newspaper benefits thereby, profiting through additional circulation and sales of other products, through an increase in prestige and good will, and by using the feedback it gets from the public to improve its contents and expand its operations.

And the way to do this, it seems to me, is by developing new products and new channels by which the tremendous information resources of the newspaper can be tapped. In our case, this means primarily the Information Bank, our computerized morgue, but obviously that sort of undertaking is not possible for most newspapers. I am not really referring to the new technological marvels of the communications industry—the day when they will enable Mrs. Jones to look up a recipe published four months ago, or when they will furnish her fourteen–year–old with details on last spring's world soccer championship, or when they will enable his teacher to flash the story of the latest Middle Eastern peace proposal on a screen in the classroom; that day is probably a generation or more away.

Meanwhile, there are other products and services we can offer, using devices and techniques already available. Material from the newspaper files can be collected by topic, reprinted by low–cost methods, and thus made available. This has always been done for articles by a given writer; but only lately has there been an attempt to offer such reprints by topic. (*The Times*, for example, now offers reprints of its Book Review supplement, of all movie reviews, and of biographical material.) Special subject collections can also be offered in recordings and in other audio-visual forms. Microphoto technology and the vast improvements in indexing techniques and index production can and should be exploited to permit the establishment of "satellite morgues" that require little storage space and whose contents can be easily tapped and duplicated.

John Rothman

The press, beset by economic pressures and well aware of its dependence on the public, is concentrating much of its energies on developing such products and services, for its own sake as well as that of the public. The public, relying on the newspaper for so much of its information and requiring ready access to the information facilities there, has an important role to play by making its specific needs known and encouraging and guiding newspapers in this endeavor.

Editor's Note: Dr. Rothman prepared this article prior to the completion of *The New York Times Information Bank*, which is now in operation and selling information service to a variety of clients everywhere.

10

Public Relations in Special Libraries

Elizabeth Ferguson

Elizabeth Ferguson retired in 1969 after twenty–five years as librarian of the Institute of Life Insurance, New York City. In 1970 she was elected to the Special Libraries Association Hall of Fame. She was graduated from Oberlin College and received her degree in library science from Western Reserve University. She has been an instructor and lecturer on special libraries at Queens College, New York, Pratt Institute, Columbia University, and other institutions. She is coauthor of the volume *Creation and Development of an Insurance Library,* and editor of *Sources of Insurance Statistics.*

The public relations problems of special libraries really start with the question of defining a special library. Sadly enough, there is misunderstanding on this point, even within the library profession. I am afraid special librarians themselves have sometimes been guilty of implying that their brand of librarianship was "special" in the sense of "superior." This has not made for cordial relations with the rest of the library world.

I submit that the error may be in applying the adjective "special" to the library, or more annoyingly, to the librarian, when it should be applied to the situation in which the library operates. A basic definition may help to clear the air and at the same time provide a frame of reference for the discussion to follow. Here is my working statement on which my course, Special Libraries, is based:

> According to the official definition of Special Libraries Association, special libraries are the libraries of "business, professional, governmental and industrial organizations [which] promote the collection, organization and dissemination of information in specialized fields." They differ widely in subject interests, in organization and in methods of service, but with a few outstanding exceptions such as the subject departments of large public or university libraries, they have the common characteristic of being *integrated units of nonlibrary* organizations.
>
> A special librarian is in the position of being a staff member and/or an executive of the organization the library serves, with the duty of managing a department that renders library and information services (1) directly adapted to the needs of the organization, (2) conforming to its policies, and (3) contributing to its purposes and objectives.

In short, special librarianship is librarianship applied and adapted to a special situation.

This, I trust, will help lay the ghost of false claims to superiority. It does tell *what* special libraries are but it does not tell *why* they are. Ruth Savord, a pioneer special librarian, supplies this historical context:

> For it was left to nineteenth century America to see the vision of books for all the people and it took a great many pioneers to bring to fruition the dreams they dreamed. But the very aim of this movement, designed as it was for all the people, made it impossible for the public library to meet the demands for more and more specialized information from administrative heads of public, quasi–public, and private corporations, of city, state, and federal bureaus, and from the professional man—an increasing number of patrons who did not want the sources, from which they could glean facts, but rather, the facts themselves.
>
> The turn of the century saw these demands met by the assembly of collections of specialized information for the care and use of the mass of print which even then was pouring from our printing presses; saw the adaption of old library methods to this new library field—special librarianship.

Very briefly, special libraries exist to expedite the process of locating and providing, from the present mass of available print, specific knowledge that is needed *on the job.* The day when any technical man can operate with a slide rule and one shelf of books is long gone. The purpose of a library is (1) to save the time of expert personnel, (2) to save the company money in buying printed matter, and (3) to produce better information more efficiently.

Having defined a special library, I must also define my concept of public relations. The expression I like best comes from Holgar J. Johnson, former President of the Institute of Life Insurance, under whom I worked for many years: "Public relations is 90 percent doing a good job and only 10 percent telling about it, important as that is."

For a special library, "doing a good job" might be stated

Elizabeth Ferguson

very simply as in the standards used in the outstanding library at the Connecticut General Life Insurance Company:

1. The library provides the material for essential research in the conduct of our business.

2. The library provides reference service to assist in essential research.

3. The library promotes its services so that employees look to it for assistance.

The criterion of success is how much and how effectively these services are actually used by the staff of the organization—those who use the library. They might appear to be a captive audience but they are an audience of intelligent individualists. They are experts in their fields with full quotas of built-in prejudices and work habits that often keep them out of the library.

Perhaps the toughest barrier, the one librarians hate to admit, is a vehement dislike of library rules. The older generation of businessmen, who admittedly have not kept up with modern library developments, particularly tend to equate a library with restrictions. But they are not the only ones. Among the special library's users there are apt to be creative people who chafe under any impediment to their thought processes. An industrial Research Manager (Merritt A. Williamson of the Burroughs Corporation) put this case strongly to an audience of special librarians:

Engineers and scientists resent being told by a librarian what they can and cannot do. Try to avoid citing rules if possible. If you have to do it, try to show the benefit to them in the long run by conforming. Few of the really good workers have any respect for a rule as such but they may respect the reason for it.

He further insisted that you don't get in trouble by breaking rules occasionally—that old library bugaboo, "everybody will expect it," simply doesn't hold. He also offered some neat versions of the democratic process:

It is paramount that all persons should be treated
equitably. This does not mean, however, that they
should all be treated alike . . . . Don't *take* them seriously, but do *treat* them seriously.

Another barrier that comes as a shock is the fact that people
turn to all manner of sources other than the library for a great
deal of the information they need. First and foremost there is
the universal impulse to call old Joe who might know something
about whatever the problem is. This is not necessarily a lazy-
man's method. Old Joe may be, and often is, a learned scientific
colleague or a top financier who can produce information not
yet in print. Beside personal contacts, people often turn directly
to trade associations, the trade press, professional consultants,
research institutes, and government agencies, to mention only a
few possible sources.

Naturally these non-users must be wooed and it can't be
done overnight. A regular bulletin of new books and articles (to
be discussed below) may ring a bell at some point. So may a piece
of literature in line with his known special interest sent directly
to him. But the best method is probably to go all out with the
answer to his first request. Nothing works like demonstration.

A passing word should probably be said about the secretary
who can be a barrier or an invaluable friend. It's difficult enough
to have reference requests channeled through a second party
even when the question is reasonably clear. It becomes a major
problem when the secretary garbles the question, sometimes
doesn't know how to spell the key word or name, and definitely
doesn't want to go back to the boss for clarification. This, of
course, is an occasion for the utmost in tactful human relations.
Sometimes you know the boss well enough to call him directly,
naturally embarrassing the secretary as little as possible, or a
memo may work better. However, libraries offer a lot of help to
secretaries in the normal course and in turn a friendly secretary
can get you the boss's ear sometime or retrieve that current
journal from his desk when someone else is screaming for it.

The finest reference service in the world will be ineffective

Elizabeth Ferguson

if it doesn't take into account these human aspects, the many things that condition a user's attitude toward the library. The user must never feel embarrassed to ask for information. He should be sure that it is the library's business to locate and provide material and ideas he needs but not to infringe on his standing as an expert in his field. Comfortable surroundings in the library and an attitude of pleasant helpfulness on the part of the library staff also play an important part in creating the right atmosphere.

There are human aspects on the library side as well. Chief among them is the nonvisibility of the library in the midst of executive concerns and the so-called productive or creative activities of the organization. And for the librarian, there is what William H. Whyte, Jr. in *The Organization Man* called "anonymity of achievement."

It is logical to think of coping with the problem of nonvisibility by way of some sort of publicity communication to the staff. What is needed is a regular reminder that the library is there. A periodic bulletin with up-to-date information content is a frequent solution. Information content of genuine interest and relevance to the organization's concerns is of the essence. Promotional messages of the "use your library" type serve very little purpose.

The greatest public relations benefits can probably be reaped from a really good current news bulletin. The idea is to say in effect to busy people, "In the library we scan newspapers and magazines as they come in and we have sifted out these articles so you can review them quickly." Of course selection is the key —truly pertinent material with a neat balance between the obviously important, with which people may be already familiar, and related material from sources that might be missed. Frequency is essential for news value—weekly is probably the average although some brave libraries undertake a daily issue. Formats vary. Almost all daily bulletins, for instance, consist of mounted and xeroxed clippings with the pages stapled together under a cover sheet. A weekly publication can have a more attractive style. Processed, lettersize sheets are the usual because they fit into the office pattern. An easily identifiable logo that says "library" clearly is about all the glamorizing needed. Title listings seem to be most popular. Short annotations are desirable if time allows. There should also be a well thought out plan for providing copies of the articles on request, either by lending the publication or by furnishing xerox copies.

That hardy perennial, the list of new books, has visibility value too. In fact it is probably the most common publication effort of special libraries. It usually carries a title as simple as "Acquisition List" (which is what they actually are called) or "Books Received in the Library in October." The material is easily compiled from acquisition records. They need not be as frequent as the news bulletin to be useful. Grouping the books according to subjects or a classification is helpful in long lists. The same practices as the news bulletin as to format and follow–up provision are usually followed. Sometimes new book lists appear as a regular feature in the company magazine.

Although bulletins keep the name of the library appearing on desks regularly, there is a long tradition in special libraries for direct communication with individual staff members. One of the great rewards of a special library situation is the opportunity to know users on a long–term basis. This makes it possible to know their special interests and responsibilities. So when, in the course of his regular reviewing of incoming publications and advance notices, something appears with specific value to one individual user, the librarian calls it to that person's attention. This service can be done formally or casually as circumstances and personalities indicate. If the communication is written, it goes without saying that attractive memo forms and bookmark tabs identifying the library add a public relations touch.

I have discussed communications with users in relatively simple terms to emphasize the public relations aspects. My suggestions are really reference services, of course. So I should probably mention that the more sophisticated reference services have the same public relations values. For instance, in a technical organization a bulletin of technical abstracts might be far more apropos than a news bulletin. It is possible to purchase or photocopy journals and circulate these as information bulletins. And the universal special library practice of sending notices to individual users has graduated in machine circles to SDI, Selective Dissemination of Information.

Mr. Whyte of *The Organization Man* suggests an offbeat idea for coping with the anonymity that beclouds so much professional work in an organization. He calls it publicizing for the wrong reasons:

> It would be nice if one could sell intelligence on its real merit, but candor should force us to admit that many of our achievements in staff or professional work must be over the dead bodies of our superiors . . . . We must be very keen to merchandise the aspects of our particular specialty that are most attractive to our superiors, so that thereby we may keep the most basic things intact.

Here are some examples of public relations sidelines that have been used by special libraries. Librarians in the insurance business have found that it pays to enroll in the technical insurance courses required of other staff—it speeds their grasp of the subject matter and allies them with their users in a nice way. Many companies nowadays are engaged in programs of community social service and they welcome participation by their librarians. A lending collection of general reading books and records is a great asset under some circumstances, as in the case of a company in an isolated location. This latter is to be thought of as a personnel service, however, and must have high–level clearance and financial support.

As an administrator, the special librarian stands in a dual position: (1) he is part of the management setup of the organization itself, and (2) he is the direct administrator of the library functions. In his relationships with his users he is functioning as the direct administrator. One might well say that he is performing that ninety percent of public realtions—"doing the job"—with a sensitivity to individual needs.

The librarian's position as a member of the management staff of his organization entails a different kind of responsibility. Basically this responsibility is to see the library from management's point of view. It has always been popular among professionals to think of management, the establishment in today's parlance, as something apart, the enemy in fact. But, since he himself is part of it, the librarian must be able to fit the library function into the overall operation of the organization, to think like management, in other words.

On the organization chart the library shows as a staff or service unit. Staff departments exist to provide advice and service to the line which is the chain of command directly responsible for accomplishing the objectives of the organization. It is a hard fact of life that service groups rate as overhead, as nonproductive in an accounting sense. Since they cannot show a profit, they have a never–ending responsibility to justify the amounts of money it takes to run them, to show that they are pulling their weight in the work of the organization.

Within the chain of command, the librarian reports to a designated officer who is the library's link to top management. This officer is the captain of the library team. The ultimate responsibility for the success or failure of the library rests with him. Now and again one hears a special librarian say happily, "My boss is very library–minded," and all honor to those true believers. They have done much to further the library cause. For the most part, however, the officer is a businessman without specific library background and the library is only one of his several responsibilities.

Under these circumstances it is not surprising that one often hears special librarians say that their major problem is to "educate management." I submit, however, that there is a most unattractive air of superiority in this phrase, and I would like to see it eliminated from our public relations vocabulary. *Inform, interpret*—yes—but not *educate.*

Elizabeth Ferguson

The fate of the library literally depends on effective communication between librarian and officer, and the burden of initiating and maintaining the interchange falls squarely on the shoulders of the librarian. To ease the burden somewhat, it is only fair to point out that the officer, too, has a stake in a successful library. His reputation depends on the performance of the units under him. It is worth any amount of effort to put him in the position not only of backing the library but talking about it with understanding and enthusiasm.

Before getting into the ways and means of pursuing this vital communication, I want to say an earnest word about the hazards in library terminology. There should be a categorical rule: Don't use it. It is a real barrier to mutual understanding. Learning to describe library operations in plain English can be surprisingly difficult for librarians, but mastering the art pays big dividends. These paragraphs from the position description of the librarian at the Connecticut General Life Insurance Company are well phrased to give a nonlibrarian a good picture of what a librarian does:

1. Selects books, periodicals and other material to be added to Library, aiming to select the best from a mass of literature, through appraisal of book reports, discussion with company personnel or other librarians, review of book itself, and relying upon knowledge of publishers, book reports and authors. Anticipates needs of departments on new developments, new products, trends and periodic demand.

2. Provides answers to a great variety of questions of executives and employees in Home Office and Field. This normally requires the selective furnishing of reference material, analyzing or summarizing such material and frequently requires research. Catalogues and develops systems for maintaining library materials in such a way as to facilitate searching.

Parenthetically, I might note that a common ground in language seems to be developing by way of automation. Machine terms are pretty common nowadays. I suspect that using them may offer subtle proof that the library has come out of its dusty past and is now with it. Any librarians should know by now that it is quite easy to describe library processes in machine terms even when machines aren't actually in use. This may indeed be a useful pattern in the future.

The librarian's first line of communication is the regular business of running the library—everything from budgets to personnel problems that needs the officer's authority or his counsel. A few thoughtful rules that are really just good business practice make for good public relations here. Being considerate of the boss's time heads the list. From our Research Manager again:

> Try to let him know in advance what you have on your mind and give him a time estimate of your needs. Give him a list of your topics arranged in order of importance. Any boss appreciates a person who is considerate of his time.

And when it comes to making proposals:

> If you have an idea you want to promote, don't just wander into the boss's office. Formulate a carefully thought out plan of action. Give him a proposal which he can approve. He isn't going to approve anything vague or verbal. Whether you like the thought or not, you are a salesman although you are selling something intangible.

Mr. Williamson's "proposal" obviously means "problem with solution." And he would agree, I'm sure, that the magic formula for promoting any library project is to show how it will benefit the company.

The officer depends on the librarian to keep him informed about important things going on in the library. This duty can be turned to good public relations account. It offers the golden opportunity to interpret the library.

The most obvious avenue for informing management is the formal report, and this can be a pretty sore subject among busy

Elizabeth Ferguson

librarians. Oddly enough, part of the problem is that they are not universally required of special libraries. So one hears an interesting variety of comments: "My management wouldn't read a report." "All my people care about is statistics." "I send my boss monthly reports even though he doesn't ask for them—I want him to know what we're doing." "My reports are included in the company's annual report."

There is a lot to say in favor of the report. Most important, it is a basic part of the officer's upward communication in the hierarchy and it must come from the library. It is also an occasion for the librarian to take stock and review the progress of the library. Reports should include periodically a review of the objectives of the library with emphasis on how the objectives further the interests of the organization. Repetition of such basics is necessary and valuable since executives change and memories are short. A report gives the factual record of the library's accomplishment. A librarian is well advised, by the way, to keep this factual record whether or not a report is done regularly—one can never tell when statistics may be suddenly required.

Any efforts to make a report interesting and readable pay good dividends. An occasional illustrative story about a library job adds life and individuality to the bare facts. It is a great comfort at report time to have a daybook record or a folder of notes of such illustrative material accumulated throughout the year. This could include notes of special jobs or interesting contacts, letters, writings produced, staff accomplishments—the sort of thing that doesn't show up in regular records.

Of course the best stories are to be found in the reference jobs that are the library's raison d'etre. Reporters, for instance, always consider "funny questions" good copy. In fact, I confess that for several years I too believed we should feature stories about our reference exploits in publicizing special libraries. This idea came out of a Public Relations Clinic sponsored by Special Libraries Association in the early 1950s in which I was much involved.

I have since come to think that it is rather questionable taste to make capital of these stories. A reference question, we should remember, is somebody's problem. In a public library situation it may be possible to phrase questions discreetly so as to give interesting examples without violating confidence or, unforgivably, holding up to ridicule. In a special library one lives with the questioners and telling their stories amounts to claiming credit for part of a man's work. It's not a good way to win friends. And there are the further hazards that one might be giving away a business secret or that the results of the research may have backfired.

Our Research Manager comes down hard on this point:

> The value of nearly every service department to the overall organization is inversely proportional to the amount of credit it claims for its contributions. I do not believe that the library is an exception to this.

This is a very sensitive aspect of the anonymity problem, of course. And I hasten to say that special librarians usually suffer their anonymity in silence rather than risk talking out of turn. In spite of my caution, however, I do believe that there are times and circumstances when the reference story can be told appropriately and gracefully. Marian Lechner, for instance, in a talk to insurance executives selected one about a project well known in the company and with the library's role clearcut:

> Last month Connecticut General sponsored a television program in the Who, What, Why, Where, When series entitled "The Heritage of Apollo." Constantinos Doxiades, the Greek urban planner, was featured in that program. Exactly six and a half working days before the program was aired, our advertising department requested us to assemble a library display containing all the books and magazine articles written by and about Mr. Doxiades.
>
> An exhibit such as this is a part of our company philosophy of keeping employees informed. In our li-

Elizabeth Ferguson

brary we found some fifteen magazine articles. We owned none of the books and we were able to find only one we could borrow. But we were able to identify and buy four of his books in New York and have them and the periodicals on hand within two and a half days so the display could be set up a week before the program.

It is also proper to give a supervisor, for his better understanding, information that would not be used for publicity. Even here the stricture against claiming undue credit holds, but there are little ways and means. The occasional memo headed "you might like to know" or "to keep you posted" is one of the best vehicles. Businessmen do go through their in–boxes and at their own choice of time, so this is a way to get library news into the mainstream of office communication.

The same kinds of things that have been suggested for report material adapt well to memos. The possibilities are endless—a note of appreciation for service given (third party endorsement is always acceptable); a much–needed but hard–to–get information source obtained through interlibrary loan (to show the value of library contacts); brief interesting reports of meetings attended (pointing out information and contacts useful to the company); notice of an office or honor in a library association (being sure to explain what the association is, i.e., the New York Chapter of SLA represents 1200 libraries in this area); a new staff manual (this can be not only an evidence of efficiency but also quite descriptive of what goes on in the library).

In all this discussion of the library in the chain of command, it has been necessary to emphasize the official role of the librarian as background for public relations activities. The library staff plays an important role as well. The staff, as we have seen, is a key factor in the library's relationships with library users. It is vital to the total effort that the staff be continuously informed as to important management policies and decisions, and this is a further responsibility of the librarian.

Outside its own organization there is a public of vital concern to the special library—that is, other libraries and librarians. One of the characteristic features of a special library is that it has a selective and limited collection and must depend on outside resources fairly frequently. This makes interlibrary exchange and cooperation a matter of everyday concern since another byword of a special library is that it cannot say "Sorry, we don't have that information."

The exchange among special librarians has an informal, person–to–person quality that is not often found in other parts of the library world. It is based on personal acquaintance with the resources and specialties of special libraries, especially those within a given area. Its saving grace is that it is reciprocal. It is such an asset to a library's reference service that it has been called the special librarian's "secret weapon." And this access to outside resources is one of the library's strong points with management.

Any such interchange can flourish only in a friendly, pleasant climate. The courtesies become very important. Much of the business is conducted over the telephone, since the information is often wanted "yesterday," and library staffs must be trained not only to ask questions clearly but to use good telephone manners. Acknowledgments of the service are excellent public relations. Many libraries have effective "returned with thanks" forms, and a personal note is often in order. A librarian once told me that she went to the SLA Chapter Christmas party for the purpose of saying thank you in person to people who had helped her during the year. Christmas cards with the same message are also a nice gesture and are used quite frequently.

I regret to say, however, that there is another side to the interlibrary relations picture that is not all sweetness and light, that, in fact, has a rather stormy history. I refer to the relations between special libraries and university and research libraries. It is only to be expected that a special library serving research people at some time is going to be asked for a paper from an obscure journal that only a huge, comprehensive collection would have. Obtaining such items is one of the signal services a special library can offer its clientele. And over the years the research libraries have made their wealth available magnificently.

Elizabeth Ferguson

The majority of the transactions are carried through smoothly.

Problems arise when overuse by special libraries interferes with the research library's service to its own clientele. This can happen when too much material is out on interlibrary loan and not available, or when the staff of the research library must take an undue amount of time to verify requests submitted with incomplete or incorrect information. There have been crisis situations in some areas that have posed serious public relations problems to SLA chapters. Columbia University and the New York Public Library have discussed the matter at several New York Chapter meetings. And a situation that began with the wartime pressures on the libraries of the Southern California aircraft plants is still not resolved. The ALA Interlibrary Loan Code is a direct outgrowth of this latter crisis.

One way to alleviate the problem is, of course, for the lending library to establish a system of fees. There is a small trend in this direction and it is likely to become more common. Although amply justified in theory, it is difficult to practice and demands adjustments on both sides.

It obviously doesn't do the image of the special librarian any good to be called a "parasite," yet this term has appeared in some of the published discussions of this problem. At this point in time two efforts need to be made. The first is a kind of holding action. Librarians must conduct all interlibrary loan transactions with scrupulous regard for the rules and time limits of the lending library. As far as possible they must do the bibliographic work themselves. Further, they should make a real effort to spread the load of requests among the many specialized libraries instead of overusing a few. This requires more work, but it is often possible.

The second effort should be to keep informed about and, where possible, to participate in the formalized interlibrary cooperative systems that are being set up throughout the library world. It's becoming a truism to say that in this day of overwhelming masses of information materials and unprecedented demands on them, no library can live alone. And cooperation goes far beyond interlibrary loan—it can involve cooperative buying, exchange of materials and services, and rules for the mutual use of libraries.

It isn't going to be easy for special librarians to find their proper role in these systems. There are strictures, for example, against having representatives of profit-making companies on the boards of library organizations supported by government funds. Or special librarians may understandably wonder whether the local college library will want to send a whole class with a special assignment to work in their small, crowded library. Or the company will insist on knowing "what's in it for us" when asked to pay for a membership in a library cooperative. These are just a few of the roadblocks that will come up.

Special libraries do owe a debt to the rest of the library world. They do have spectacular information resources in specialized fields of knowledge. It would be useful to make these resources more widely available for research needs if ways and means could be found for removing the roadblocks. Difficulties, it seems to me, tend to be aggravated when dealings between libraries are forced into the rigid mold of a mechanized system. Perhaps the systems would work better if they allowed for the person-to-person approach that special librarians have used so successfully for so many years. The cooperative systems are coming in one way or another. They may prove to be a challenging public relations opportunity for special libraries. If special librarians really join the library community on a contributing basis, they can certainly disavow the charge of "parasite" and make the title "special librarian" mean what it should—a librarian working in a special situation with access to special resources.

Elizabeth Ferguson

Bibliography on Public Relations in Special Libraries

The sources cited in this chapter are included in this listing. The additional references offer different points of view and many specifics of special library experience with various media and techniques for public relations activities.

Bill, E.C. "What to Do. . . How to Do It. . . When You Take an Idea to Top Management." *Sales Management*, 58 (1957): 29–30.

Brown, Alberta L. "Relation of the Librarian to Management, to the Patron, and to the Library." *Bulletin of the Medical Library Association*, 46 (1958): 82–90.

——."Working Smarter with your Clientele." *Special Libraries,* 49 (1958): 431–433.

Drucker, Peter F. "How to Be an Employee." *Fortune Magazine*, 45 (May 1952): 26 ff.

Ferguson, Elizabeth. "Librarian and the Organization Man." *Special Libraries*, 50 (1959): 367–372.

——. "Special Librarians Need Not Be Parasites." *Library Journal*, 59 (1959): 3372–3375.

——. *Special Libraries.* (course outline)

——. "What, Why and How of Annual Reports." *Special Libraries*, 47 (1956): 203–206.

Fisher, Eva L. *Checklist for the Organization, Operation and Evaluation of a Company Library*. New York, Special Libraries Association, 1966. (Sections O, P, Q, R.)

Lechner, Marian G. "How One Company Describes and Pays Librarians." *Special Libraries*, 52 (1961): 455–458.

Medical Library Association. *Handbook of Medical Library Practice.* 2nd ed. Chicago, American Library Association, 1956. (pp. 239–261)

Pearce, Catherine A. "Public Relations." *Business and Finance Division Bulletin, Special Libraries Association*, 4 (April 1962): 8–24.

Raburn, Josephine. "Public Relations for a 'Special Public.'" *Special Libraries*, 60 (1969): 647–650.

Sass, Samuel. "Must Special Librarians Be Parasites?" *Special Libraries*, 50 (1959): 149–154.

Savord, Ruth. *Special Librarianship as a Career.* New York, Special Libraries Association, 1955.

Sharp, Harold S. *Readings in Special Librarianship.* New York, Scarecrow Press, 1963. (pp. 293–336)

Special Libraries Association. *Every Special Librarian Should Have a Public Relations Program.* New York, The Association, 1953.

Strauss, Lucille K., Strieby, Irene M., and Brown, Alberta L. *Scientific and Technical Libraries, Their Organization and Administration.* New York, Interscience Publishers, 1964. (Chapter 12)

Strieby, Irene M. "Public Relations Activities of Special Libraries." *Library Trends,* 7 (1958): 290–297.

Towner, Isabel L. "Compiler." *Directory of Special Libraries.* New York, Special Libraries Association, 1953. (Ferguson, Elizabeth. Introduction)

Wells, Marion. "Public Relations." *Special Libraries,* 41 (Transactions, 1950): 55–56.

Williamson, Merritt A. "How to Get Along with your Bosses." 1956. (Unpublished manuscript.)

11

Technology, Libraries, and Public Relations

Howard Hitchens, Jr.

Howard Hitchens, Jr. is Executive Director of the Association for Educational Communications and Technology. He holds a B.A. from the University of Delaware, an M.A. from Teachers College, Columbia University, and a Ph.D. in Instructional Communications from Syracuse University. He served in the United States Air Force for twenty–six years, flying combat missions in the Pacific and Korea. He was for four years at the Air Force Academy as Chief of the Film and Television Division of Audiovisual Services. He was also Associate Professor and Director of the media program at the Air Force Academy from 1959 to 1969. Before assuming his present post, he was a member of the board of directors of the AECT.

Everybody knows what a library is. It's a place where they keep books; it's a place where I can go to study; it's a place where I can find statistical information that I need for my job; it's a place where I can find quiet for relaxation and escape from the cacophony of the workaday world; it's where Marian hangs out; it's a place that increasingly has all sorts of things in it in addition to books; it's an idea; it's an information storage and retrieval center; it's our community center and meeting place.

The "library" is probably all of those things and more if a sample poll were taken of the general citizenry of the country. But let's examine the library in the educational setting—how it functions, how it might relate to its "public."

The library that is embedded in educational settings these days is a *part of the technology of education.* That is my argument in defining the library, and it is from that viewpoint that I undertake a discussion of the ways in which the technological environment called an educational institution can seek a relationship with the public it serves.

Ours is a technological society. What does that mean? It means that America is in the postindustrial revolution, a most sophisticated age in which man has a very complex relationship with his environment.

It has been said that technology is the "ordering of the possessions of the human mind." This is a short way of stating the intent of Charles A. Beard in 1932:

> What then is this technology which constitutes the supreme instrument of modern progress? Although the term is freely employed in current writings, its meaning as actuality and potentiality has never been explored and defined. Indeed, so wide–reaching are its ramifications that the task is difficult and hazardous. Narrowly viewed, technology consists of the totality of existing laboratories, machines, and processes already developed, mastered, and in operation. But it is far more than mere objective realities.
>
> Intimately linked in its origin and operation with pure

science, even its most remote mathematical speculations, technology has a philosophy of nature and method—an attitude toward materials and work—and hence is a subjective force of high tension. It embraces within its scope great constellations of ideas, some explored to apparent limits and others in the form of posed problems and emergent issues dimly understood.[1]

John Kenneth Galbraith in his *The New Industrial State* (1967) defines technology as the "systematic application of scientific or other organized knowledge to practical tasks. Its most important consequence, at least for purposes of economics, is enforcing the division and subdivision of any such task into its component parts. Thus, and only thus, can organized knowledge be brought to bear on performance."

One of the earliest technological developments having to do with human learning and the transmission of knowledge from generation to generation was the invention of the printing press by Gutenberg. At the time of its development, many scholars and pedagogs decried the advent of this print technology as heralding the demise of education. Obviously it had an exactly opposite effect—it heralded the rise of the availability of an education to the entire citizenry in the western world. And it was largely the printing press that supported the evolution of that most technological concept in human communications—the library.

Therefore, in the education setting the library must be viewed for what it is—a very complex and sophisticated respository of stored information which, if it is functioning properly, can serve as an efficient and effective information storage and retrieval center. Do we introduce technology into the library? Have we introduced technology into the library? Obviously we do and we have.

But at the same time, in the educational setting the library is a part of the technology itself. There is, in fact, a particular technology that is central to the functioning of any educational institution, be it an elementary school, a volunteer–operated

202   Howard Hitchens, Jr.

kindergarten, a graduate school, a multiversity, or an industrial training establishment. That central concern is instruction; and it is the instructional technology that is of overwhelming importance in today's education setting.

What is instructional technology? In the words of the report of the President's Commission on Instructional Technology in 1969, it is "A systematic way of designing, carrying out and evaluating the total process of learning and teaching in terms of specific objectives, based on research in human learning and communication, and employing a combination of human and non-human resources to bring about more effective instruction."[2]

A great number of professionals in the field of library science have come to equate the term "communications media" with technology. Obviously the tools that allow a medium to be used for human communication are products of our advanced technology. For instance, the motion picture projector is a very sophisticated device which is necessary in order to use the film medium for communication. But that product of our complex technology is not technology itself; again, the technology is a process. It is a "systematic way . . ."

The library as a part of the communications technology and as a human institution deserves closer examination. Most of us are familiar with the Dewey Decimal and Library of Congress cataloging system argument. This argument goes, indeed, much deeper than merely whether one set of symbols is more efficient from a physiological standpoint for the user and cataloger to manipulate. It goes to the heart of the matter as far as the library science is concerned—the question of the ability of that symbol system to order the entire body of human knowledge that has accumulated down through the ages in the most useful way to allow a person access to it.

Many information scientists have toyed with the idea of putting this information in some other symbol form so that it can be more efficiently retrieved and more effectively used. So far they have been stymied. There have been some rather spectacular efforts made and many scientific endeavors are still underway. The storage of information in thermoplastics, the reducing of the verbal symbol system to a digital system in electronic data processing form, and storing information on magnetic tape or some other electromechanical form still hold some promise.

In his provocative book, Ben H. Bagdikian poses the question of whether twenty years from now we will still be reading a morning newspaper, or "Will computerized news be transmitted by coaxial cable to your home, where you'll make copies of items you want to examine, then press a button for further information?"

You'll note that print is not discarded in his speculation. In fact, print as a means of communicating is far from dying. As Mr. Bagdikian observes, "In five hundred years the speed of setting type rose from one line a minute to fourteen lines a minute in 1960. In 1966, 1800 lines became possible, and one year later a machine appeared that can set 15,000 lines a minute. That very high speed machine isn't widely used and may never be."[3]

So the changeover of the traditional library as a book repository to some completely transformed electronic marvel will probably not take place in our lifetime. In the words of the Educational Facilities Laboratory, "technological developments in the foreseeable future will not alter radically the way libraries are used. In planning library buildings today, we should start with the library as the institution we now know it to be. Any departure in the future should be made from this firm base."[4]

Whether this reflects more the conservatism of a venerable institution or an objective, accurate assessment of the situation in the last third of the twentieth century remains to be seen.

Let us turn now from a speculative gaze into the future to the realities of the present. As the technological center of the academic institution, an entity that is primarily concerned with human communication, how can the library (learning resources center, media center, instructional communciations center) use a public relations program to further its purposes and those of

Howard Hitchens, Jr.

the educational environment in which it serves? There are many ways. The most obvious way in which the information storage and retrieval center can serve its public is by educating its users to make the best use of its capabilities. This place has changed; it does have, normally, a listening center of some kind for its patrons; it does have a place for holding cultural events—be they small concerts, poetry readings, book talks; it does have the capacity to display works of art; it does have the capacity to display informational exhibits and current information in various interesting fashions. The physical arrangement of the information storage and retrieval center itself can facilitate serving a multitude of patrons.

But let's pay some attention to the possibility of the library as a part of the technology of the educational institution in serving as a bridge between the community at large and the learners (be they children, teenagers, or adults). Public cooperation is the foundation of that bridge.

The general purpose to be served by a public relations program for the technology program of any educational institution must be to secure the cooperation of the public served by that institution. There is a general information component to that purpose which cannot be denied. Any education manager worth his salt recognizes the need for a general public relations program to provide information for the surrounding citizenry so that his educational institution will be able to function in a comfortable climate. Furthermore, not only must the psychological climate in the community be a comfortable one for the institution, there must be positive support generated for the program of that institution.

The most successful philosophy to adopt in building an aura of acceptance on the part of the citizenry is to aim toward a cooperative effort with the community in achieving the ends of education generally and of the institution in particular. There are six main levels of activity in which there can be citizen cooperation in education. These are: studying (including the assembling of data), planning, interpreting, deciding, executing, and evaluating.

Technology, Libraries, and Public Relations 205

Just as in examining any community problem, the first level of activity is that of *studying* the problem—*assembling data* concerning the problem. A cooperative stance that enlists the aid of citizens out of the community to assist in collecting data about a problem will work provided that the problem is clearly defined and the public, in the form of a committee or some other ad hoc group, understands the problem. In a general library the problem might be that there are not enough fiction titles on the shelves to satisfy the requirements of the community's readers, or, there are not enough reference sources available to the people who want to do research in the community. A similar problem in the educational library might be the development of an advisory committee for the comparison of costs for equipping or expanding the facilities of the school plant. Once the group of cooperative citizens has been enticed into serving on such a committee and the task defined, their advice probably should be sought. However, it should be clearly pointed out that their work is finished once they have collected the information.

The next cooperative activity possible is that of *planning*. Again, the advisory group is made privy to the aims and purposes of the institution so that they can assist in the planning. If, as in the case of a community college, the advisory group represents all segments of the community's society, it determines the aims and purposes. Such a group might in its planning consider such needs as a terminal education for vocational and technical training and the need to have middle level educational programs available for persons who may eventually want to pursue a liberal arts degree. Again, the planning might be the development of a five–year plan to support the community's needs, which have been determined in the study step of the process.

The aim of a public relations program outward from within the institution has to be, among other things, that of *interpreting* the institution's program to the community. The information storage and retrieval center of the institution obviously has a role to play in supporting this interpretive role.

206   Howard Hitchens, Jr.

The *deciding* activity can be a cooperative venture. But more likely, it is only shared minimally with those not directly responsible for the institution's progress. For example, a decision might be to use voluntary help from the local community in order to make an educational program function more effectively in a public school system. That decision must be left to the person the community has chosen to shoulder the responsibility for managing that educational institution—the superintendent, president, or dean of instruction.

The *executing* of a solution can involve the community's individuals at various levels. The volunteers themselves, for instance, could keep an instructional materials center open beyond the normal hours which tax funds can support in personnel salaries. The Parent Teachers Association or other groups which are ancillary to the educational institution but comprised of the citizenry can take the initiative frequently in providing voluntary help, donations of real goods, or money.

The *evaluation* of the institution's program and its various services, including the library, is a form of activity that can be engaged in minimally by the public. Certainly we can depend on the families of students in the educational system to provide some feedback on the efficiency and effectiveness of the educational system. But the primary responsibility for evaluation lies, of course, with the officially recognized bearers of the responsibility for managing the educational system. In the case of public education, that generally is the board of education for the public schools in the community.

The following report of a massive attempt to directly affect the taxpayers of one county in Long Island, New York, is described in sufficient detail to serve as a good example of interpreting the school's program for the community and many of the functions just discussed. Forty–seven of the local 127 school budgets in that part of Long Island had been defeated on first submission to the electors. The following in the words of Dr. David Guerin, describes exactly how he and his associates accepted the challenge:[5]

What to do? Educate the *No* voter! But how? He votes No but he doesn't read the publicity put out by the school, and never comes out to PTA meetings, board meetings, back–to–school night, open–school week, or any other occasion which would acquaint him with the aims, objectives and programs of the schools. I suggested that since he won't come to us, we go to him. We should set up an educational exposition in a place where he can't help but see it . . . in the largest shopping center on Long Island (Roosevelt Field) . . . a place where, incidentally, he goes to spend his money. The LIECC executive board agreed to take this on as the major project of the year.

This was our basic premise:

First, take a positive attitude. Believe that when the public understands that children clearly benefit from educational expenditures, more local support can be expected. Believe that the majority of the public really wants children to learn how to learn, how to think, how to inquire, how to solve problems, and how to gather information and work with it. Identify this with quality education, but don't separate it from the basic three Rs which the public would never vote against. Instead, designate the exposition as "The 3 Rs + 2 = Reasoning and Research."

Second, understand that people believe what they see with their own eyes and what they experience themselves.

Third, believe that a large, demanding project is good medicine for an organization, particularly if it joins the membership in common cause with other professional organizations. It is when all the membership is actively involved that a sense of group identity and true organizational strength is developed.

With the above beliefs to undergird its efforts, LIECC took these steps:

Howard Hitchens, Jr.

–Arranged with the shopping center to take over display space. The shopping center agreed to publicize the event in full-page ads, to supply guards and platforms, and to help develop a logo.

–Laid plans to set up a series of modules to include:

  –A complete replica of an IMC with carrels, an extensive collection of software and hardware (including 5,000 books), and a check-out counter;

  –A replica of a local production center;

  –An early childhood education center;

  –Two preview theaters;

  –A remote TV van;

  –A demonstration classroom;

  –A reception room for teachers and students;

  ˌ–An information booth.

–Set up a "3 Rs + 2" Task Force with different individuals and teams responsible for project coordination, program, correspondence, publicity, brochures, software, hardware, electrical power, personnel, security, floor plans and layout. Each module had its own separate team which was fully responsible for the operation of the module.

–Enlisted the endorsement and support of concerned educational organizations—Association of Chief School Administrators, School Boards Association, School Library Association, Public Library System, PTA, State Education Department, Board of Cooperative Educational Services, State Teachers Association, State Federation of Teachers, American Institute of Architects.

–Enlisted the cooperation of forty educational suppliers in setting up the modules and financing the exposition.

–Launched a publicity program which included: "3 Rs + 2" interviews on three radio stations, spot announcements aired throughout the day, a live broadcast from the shopping center, a TV panel on the school budget crisis taped at the shopping center for later broadcast, a supporting editorial in *Newsday*, a news release which was picked up by the *New York Daily News* and many Long Island newspapers and by publications of various professional organizations. In addition, there were full–page ads, a "3 Rs + 2" poster contest in the schools, announcements posted in the schools and made by cooperating professional groups at their meetings. A film called "Reach the Public" was shot during the exposition so the essence of what we did could be shared with others.

Meanwhile, the Task Force worked on the program and logistics. The project idea was born in June. By December, we were in high gear, to be ready for March 19–21.

The logistics of getting ready involved numerous details. Some of the most notable were:

–designing the layout for traffic flow so all activities could proceed without interfering with one another;
–designing and setting up twin preview theaters;
–determining electrical load and constructing our own electrical circuitry;
–securing drapes to separate the various areas;
–setting up adequate sound amplification at an optimum level;
–building the demonstration platform;
–securing and laying carpeting;
–putting all tables, chairs, shelving, counters, carrels, equipment, and materials in place;
–designing, writing, typing, pasting up, and having printed a brochure and program which told the philosophy of the exposition. It contained a map, a directory, and a series of supporting statements by the Association of Chief School Administrators, the

Howard Hitchens, Jr.

State Teachers Association, the State Federation of Teachers, the PTA, and the School Boards Association;

–setting up and scheduling personnel for all modules throughout the three–day period, plus personnel to serve as additional security staff;

–planning and producing signs to identify the major modules and to credit suppliers for their participation. We felt that if we were to reach the public, the entire operation had to be manned by professionals and be a re–creation of something that might reasonably exist in their own schools. In short, it must be functional and functioning. This ruled out the "exhibit" concept with booths and displays such as prevails at conventions or fairs.

Preparation for the program involved a wealth of detail. Thirteen different school districts and a university contributed demonstration classes. A total of twenty-eight different demonstration lessons were presented over the three–day period—fourteen elementary, seven secondary, six early childhood, and one K–12. Each participating teacher filled out a form which supplied information on objectives of the lesson, room arrangements, software and hardware requirements, and number of students. Many demonstrated individualization and required elaborate set–ups. Each lesson was videotaped. Scheduling was tight, with a new demonstration almost every hour. A stage crew quickly changed the set between lessons. As new groups of students arrived, they were directed to a reception area to await their turn. Transportation was provided by the schools for the most part.

In the evenings we used the demonstration platform for special presentations. Other activities were temporarily halted when the specials were on. These included "Concepts in Communication," a three–screen color presentation by Eastman Kodak; "The Day the Schools Closed," a CBS national documentary on school budget defeats; and "What is Dance?" a live ballet performance presented by the Nassau County Dance Association.

Another big programing task was the selection and scheduling of films for the two preview theaters. A total of 107 different films, chosen from the collections of ten producers, were shown over the three–day period. Projectionists were recruited from the local school districts.

Activities in the local production center were presented as public interest warranted. They included TV, 8mm, 35mm, overhead transparencies, and various types of reproduction equipment.

Activities in the IMC were not scheduled, but every effort was made to involve the public in direct interaction with the materials. Here we had the cooperation of the librarians who helped staff this module as though it were an actual IMC. They, along with our educational communications personnel, helped familiarize the public with the collection and with the associated hardware.

We operated on the conviction that providing taxpayers with a personal learning experience would make them appreciate the value of those facilities for their children. In each case, they were encouraged to actually view the film, listen to the tape, and peruse the book in an area of interest to them.

Throughout the exposition we strove for credibility. We avoided commercialism. We deliberately avoided the inclusion of glamorous and expensive items such as computer–assisted instruction and dial–access. Our aim was to present things that were clearly realizable as well as clearly desirable. We kept in mind that we were trying to turn around the *No* voter. We showed the public their own teachers and students, teaching and learning successfully, and we tried to give them a taste, too.

How did it all work out? In our thank-you letter to

212   Howard Hitchens, Jr.

all supporters and participants we put it this way:

"It remains to be seen whether we closed the communications gap sufficiently to reach our prime behavioral goal: significantly greater local support for school budgets. It is undoubtedly too much to expect of one exposition in one shopping center to completely reverse or even greatly diminish a trend, but we did succeed in communicating. Over the three days of the exposition at the Roosevelt Field Shopping Center, we gave literally thousands of people a chance to see for themselves effective teaching and effective instructional support materials and equipment. In the many interviews conducted as part of the shooting of a documentary film, the fact that the exhibit was convincing was repeatedly evidenced, but evidenced also was the correlative response that the money cupboard is getting bare. Was it convincing enough to bring about something as basic as a reordering of priorities? That we don't know. We do know, however, that we did something that was right and sorely needed."

Based on the number of brochures and programs given out over the three-day period of the exposition, attendance was at least 20,000. This was encouraging. Even more encouraging was that come budget vote time, despite confident predictions that the number of school budget defeats would continue to rise, there were fewer. In the prior year, 47 Long Island school budgets out of 127 had been defeated on first submission, after "3 Rs + 2" there were 39 . . . ."

Obviously, the Long Island educators were very ambitious; but they did some things right. A fairly comprehensive list of guides for carrying out a cooperative program that will point the way to good decisions has existed for a number of years and goes as follows:

Participating groups and committees
1. Should understand their functions and limitations
2. Should have latitude to explore all possibilities included in assigned problems
3. Should organize properly for effective work
4. Should select individuals who believe in cooperative endeavor for leadership roles
5. Should adopt a written statement of purposes, policies, and working relations
6. Should utilize all appropriate resources
7. Should select as consultants capable persons who can work best in a cooperative program
8. Should proceed logically and scientifically
9. Should open meetings to the public
10. Should adopt a working plan with definite termination dates for aspects of their programs
11. Should meet as often as necessary to insure continuous progress
12. Should develop constructive proposals to affect improvements in the educational program
13. Should center their attention on principles and issues, not personalities
14. Should assemble evidence concerning desirable objectives or the characteristics of a desirable program should be used in evaluating the present situation
15. Should recognize the need to facilitate cooperative action in general
16. Should prepare an explanatory report giving findings and conclusions
17. Should assist in interpreting the report to the Board of Education and possibly to the public
18. Should serve principally as a policy committee when such a cooperative group is undertaking a comprehensive study

Howard Hitchens, Jr.

So much for the general public and the community *surrounding* an educational institution. Let's address ourselves to even more important "publics"—the faculty of the institution and the student body.

The faculty of the institution should be encouraged to avail itself of the services available from the technological center of the institution. How does one attract faculty into the use of the services and facilities available? Well, the services must be readily available and the physical facilities must be attractive and enticing in and of themselves. Convenient location is of prime importance. There are two or three specific activities that can be engaged in to attract the faculty's attention. In the first place, the physical facility can serve as a storage for memorabilia and as a place where materials for learning and other resources not generally available for instruction elsewhere can be made available. Exhibits can be used as both an informative tool for the casual visitor and as a means of attracting the faculty and students' attention to specific *ways* of doing things and the *products* of technology themselves.

Obviously, the technology center must be equipped with facilities for consumption of auditory and visual materials in any and all combinations. If it is, in fact, a complete communications center, it will be arranged so as to serve the audiovisual purposes so necessary to an effective program as well as for reading and other kinds of learning activities.

The learning resources center program described next is in many ways typical of the evolving school library's attempts to change itself fundamentally.

The Eastfield College campus of the Dallas Junior College District was opened for students in the fall of 1970. It is a place where change is part of a way of life. An important part of the campus, the Learning Resources Center, has come a long way from opening day, and is now beginning to deserve its name.

Central to the success of the center is its director

who is also the dean of instruction. Because of his dual role, he has been able to set for the center a different and creative stance. Although Learning Resources Center is the current "in" title for the department housing the books and media necessary for the learning process on today's campuses, it is usual to separate the different parts of the center and use the traditional terms of Library and Media Center. At Eastfield College, the names have been changed as part of a process to get faculty and students to think of the center as one place where a variety of services are provided by several people.

The Learning Resources Center exists in three parts. The Center for Independent Study is the area that many would think of as the library. Encompassing more than the traditional library, it houses a variety of materials, filmstrips, cassettes, and books, along with resources for taping, duplicating and copying material for independent use.

The Classroom Resources Center aids faculty in their instructional programs by providing equipment, technicians, films, and other manufactured resources. This area also has facilities for production of most of the art, graphics and photography needed by the college.

The third part of the LRC houses resource consultants, whose job it is to assist faculty and students in using all of the resources of the center. The three areas of the Learning Resources Center are planned to complement each other. When all come into play on a project and contribute to its successful completion, the center is doing its job.

In an effort to make the students and faculty aware of the LRC and what it offered the campus community, an LRC Week was held. The student newspaper ran a feature on the center at the beginning of the week. The feature included a discussion of the special events of LRC Week. Posters announcing the events of the week were displayed. The Friday before LRC Week, an invi-

Howard Hitchens, Jr.

tation was sent to all faculty. Included was a calendar of the week's activities.

During LRC Week itself, transparencies were projected on the walls in high–traffic areas announcing the special events of that day. The Center for Independent Study was decorated with banners and an exhibit of three–dimensional art prepared by Eastfield students. Students were recruited and introduced in detail to the facility. These students served as hosts during the Week, and acted as an effective source of information to students coming to the college for the first time.

An attempt was made to have some activity in the Center for Independent Study at all times. There were exhibits, demonstrations of equipment, a computer terminal with programed games, and a daily film festival which included a multi–media production by a group of Eastfield students. A special event was planned each day for the free period at noon. The special events incorporated faculty, students and outside speakers. The events were as varied as possible—including book reviews, a drug seminar, folk singers, a speaker on environmental and ecological issues, and a faculty music recital with singer, guitar and harpsichord.

LRC Week was a long one, filled with much activity. Everybody met a lot of people, and now the campus knows where the Learning Resources Center is and what it can do.[6]

Although libraries have always tended to provide a meeting place for cultural events in their physical facilities, today's communications center in the educational institution is taking on a more flexible character. The previously discussed cooperation works both ways; many instructional technology programs have built in the ability to use the facilities and technological products for other purposes than their library purpose of instruction. Recording entertainment activities within the academic community on videotape, and supporting other cultural events serve to interrelate the purposes of both the technologists and the academicians within the educational institution.

In short, public understanding and support of the educational institution and its instructional program can be enhanced significantly by good communication. Although the responsibility for good communication to the citizenry lies with the administration of the educational institution, a great deal can be done to develop a sense of responsibility within the community itself to communicate to its educational system or agencies. And within the system, the center of technology must insure that a strong internal communication system is at work. The world of technology within the institution must relate to the technological world that it serves.

Notes

1. Charles A. Beard, Introduction to the American edition in J. B. Bury, *The Idea of Progress* (New York: Dover, 1955, republication of 1932 Macmillan edition), pp. 22–23.

2. Sidney G. Tickton, ed., *To Improve Learning: Evaluation of Instructional Technology* (New York: Bowker, 1970), p. 7.

3. Ben H. Bagdikian, *The Information Machines: Their Impact on Men and The Media* (New York: Harper and Row, 1971), pp. 93–95.

4. *The Impact of Technology on the Library Building* (New York: Educational Facilities Laboratories, 1967), p. 19.

5. David Guerin, "Reach the Public—The 3 Rs + 2," *Audiovisual Instruction*, Vol. 16, No. 5 (May 1971).

6. Nancy Miller, "Learning Resources Center—Its Role in Education," *Audiovisual Instruction*, Vol. 16, No. 5 (May 1971).

12

Public Relations for a Developing Library
or
Starting from Scratch

Harold L. Roth

Harold Roth is Director of the Nassau County Reference Library, Garden City, New York. A graduate of New York University, he also holds a master's in library science from Columbia. He was for many years Director of the East Orange (N.J.) Public Library, and prior to that served on the staffs of the Brooklyn Public Library and the Editorial Reference Library of *The New York Times.* He has also been a lecturer in library science at Montclair (N.J.) State College and Drexel Institute Graduate School of Library Science. Before assuming his present post he was vice president in charge of library and institutional relations of the Baker & Taylor Company. He is a former president of the New Jersey Library Association.

Joseph L. Wheeler and Herbert Goldhor make the following statement in their *Practical Administration of Public Libraries* (New York: Harper and Row, 1962, p. 144): "A library's program of public relations means the concern and the activities of trustees, heads and staff members to put the library into cordial and understanding relationship with all the people of the community." This is a simple statement that embodies the total purpose of public relations. It also assumes the existence of the library, a historical base, a continuity of relationship, a staff, and some community awareness that the library exists. But in the developing library described in this paper, almost all of these elements were absent in the beginning.

Let us take a situation where the library does not exist, where plans for development stretched over a long period of time and ended in confusion, where the library community almost came to blows over the developing concept and spirits are still sensitive, where politics plays a role, where the total concept is hinged in uncertainty to a project that has lost its political glamour. Yes, all of that and more, stretching from a time of plenty to a sudden rebirth of interest as the economy goes down, arriving at a time when 25 percent of the new unemployed are the educated people who might have supported the institution, when the tax burden is becoming excessive and the entire political picture is about to change.

This is the case with the institution under discussion, and it is complicated by the fact that the director is the only professional employee, the library community is a highly organized one, competition for support is a way of life, and there is fear that a new institution may become an octopus that will gobble up any constituent libraries that may cooperate in the development of the new library.

Another significant fact is that the library concept is new. The new institution tends to be an imposed institution. As a Johnny–come–lately it is the agency which, by being last in, is the one more than likely to be frowned upon by newly united forces that resent any new agency joining the group feeding from the same trough.

If an agency is going to stay around, it is necessary that it fill a need. The need it fills need not be a need felt by all of the communities to be served. It might conceivably fill the need of only one person in a position to want something physically produced that can be pointed to as his contribution to the improvement of his constituency. Whatever the reason for the need, it becomes necessary to analyze the total situation and then to determine the steps to be taken. It becomes necessary to sharpen one's antenna and even to be opportunistic. These are all elements of public relations.

It is necessary to remember that the reason for development may also be based on true requirements. The impetus leading to ultimate completion of the agency and, on the other hand, the responsibility for making certain that it serves the public need may be found in different quarters. In the library field, the first requirement is "Know your library."

A library agency to be developed must be studied completely. In the case of the Nassau County Reference Library, the literature in papers and studies is voluminous. The study started in advance of beginning any actions and required a piecing together of each of the story lines, making certain that when an agency is mentioned its name is excerpted and set aside on a list of involved agencies or involved people. The number of mentions ticked off often led to identifying the significant trouble points that needed to be examined more closely, along with the supporting agencies.

The literature in this case consisted of files of the supporting group, the base agency developing a cultural center, similar files in the hands of an apparatus type of library agency, a member of the State 3R's Council, similar files in the Systems Headquarters library director's office; similar files in the New York State Division of Library Development office; and files in the public relations consultant's office, as well as later board minutes. Newspaper clipping files were nonexistent.

After this literature has been studied and lists have been made up, it then becomes necessary to interview significant involved persons as noted after reading the material. Questions

Harold L. Roth

arise from the reading as to the "how" and "why" of the actions taken historically.

In the process much of a personal nature comes out first. Personal likes and dislikes, although relevant, tend to distort one's point of view. Objectivity requires awareness of the tendency to develop personal bias, and requires constant testing and retesting of hypotheses and assumptions. In a situation in which the person doing the testing and studying is working alone, it becomes necessary to broaden the study base, and to cross check the evidence on a comparison graph in order to weed out obvious bias, planned distortion, and in some cases, the kind of outright antipathy that leads to skewed evidence.

Out of this study, from experiences, comes a picture that enables one to start making some decisions. Even out of the personnel files, an evaluation of the curriculum vitae of applicants leads to an understanding of trustees' concepts and the direction in which the agency's movement would get the most support from the Board.

If the word "opportunism" springs to mind, you may be correct. Nevertheless, if one does not, in making decisions, apply some intuitive opportunistic decision making, one has no real way of balancing the scales to develop an agency which, while needed for a long time, could be kept dangling for an even longer time.

What becomes apparent at this point is that with all of the literature and all of the background, there is no real history of relationship to the community. There isn't any evidence of past action in the development of such an institution because this is a *first*! Nobody has attempted the action before, even unsuccessfully. That, added to the fact that the institution itself is one that is coming into being twenty years after it was first needed and that might just be looked upon as a threat, makes the whole problem of handling public relations exactly that—a problem. (And to some of those involved, an unnecessary problem.) It also makes public relations an integral part of library administration right from the beginning. Every action must be figured in terms of building a base so that support can be assured at the time the novelty wears off and it becomes apparent that this new creature is hungry, that it is a major activity with tremendous input and support needed for personnel and expenses, year after year, even after the base collection and services have been developed.

The Board of Trustees is a valuable adjunct to a library's development. It, or a similar agency providing buffer actions, tends to make professional functions achievable. In this case, the board, which was developed to represent all phases of the support community, made the initial request for chartering of the library. It developed the connection to the state agency, hired an administration consultant to advise it on ways of receiving appropriate personnel applications, and made the request for initial staff salary. It also retained contact with the executive group of the government authority. In short, the board kept the library idea alive.

The trustees listened to their advisor and kept the initial public relations profile low in order to get the person they felt could do the total job best. It would be his responsibility to broaden the public relations approach. They set up a personnel committee to winnow the list of applicants, and they finally met as a committee–of–the–whole to make the final selections. They then carried through the processing of acceptance by the governing authority, including work with civil service. They also initiated meetings with the director of their choice, even to the point of having him develop an initial budget request and proposals for future action. With their consultant they also handled that phase of public relations—publicity—that gave the professional community information about the successful applicant that gave evidence of a start in library activity. This information was so low–keyed it appeared only in the library press, thus leaving the real public impact for the time when a building had been started.

With the hiring of an executive, the policy–making arm has every right to expect leadership and direction. The board, the policy making body in this case, is ready to provide what personal suggestions its members can supply and support wherever

Harold L. Roth

it is needed. It usually recognizes that its role, after policy and procedures are agreed upon, is a supporting one and different from that of the director. This is where the role of relation to the community begins to be shaped. The director becomes the day–to–day liaison with the government, the community, the staff and even with the board. Information is passed along either informally between meetings or more directly at meetings. The board begins to perform its major functions: serving as buffer for the library staff, providing prestige where needed in pushing programs, evaluating proposed plans, seeking support where the director does not have entree, and making it possible for the staff to develop the program.

The steps vary depending on the agency to be developed. In this case, speed was essential to the project. It was anticipated that political forces were at work in the community, with a major election scheduled. The board's desire was to have a form of operation proposed and tuned up by the time the election took place. This form of operation was to be supportable by either party. The board also helped the director in his introduction to both parties on a pleasant nonpartisan, nonpolitical basis as a professional. Commitment of intent from political candidates is important for this kind of library.

It is important to avoid building development before analyzing the needs to be served. (Buildings stand out as great contributions in a political campaign.) Even if an architect has been selected, he has to be kept at bay. The library administration has to be able to study the situation and come up with proposed solutions in every possible arena of action. The director has to be specific about some plans and vague about others. He does, however, have to push in a forward direction to show progress, but delay the building until cooperative forces can be assayed. All this must be accomplished within a restricted budget that has to be shared with three other agencies under a master budget code umbrella. The budget, normally disbursed on effective and fully justified request, is a target that is always kept in mind while direction is being shaped. Disbursement is made under top executive approval through a complicated series

A Developing Library

of maneuvers that require justification when viewed in terms of total county programs. The development of a program that can be seen as a part of the total county program is required.

This is the time the library executive develops a tentative philosophy for the library, a statement of purposes, interim objectives, and proposed long–range objectives. With the acceptance of these by the board or other policy–making body, the library is in business. It is now moving forward in an orderly direction. In this case, the philosophy and objectives become the guide that enables the board to work with the director's budget and to check on the steps involved in the library's development. It also enables the board to visualize more broadly the scope of the library building that will eventually need to be supported and fought for. This last developed from a proposal to cooperate with other large library agencies and to propose inclusion of some of their costly services in the new building, and eventually to house them in the main center to avoid replication and duplication.

During this process, and even somewhat earlier, it became necessary to be introduced to members of the immediate governing family. This too required an understanding of the agencies involved—an understanding of the lines of authority, lines of approval, and some of the freedom or lack of it that develops from the form of government in operation. A word of caution, at this point. Each government tends to have its own method of action, and steps by which one moves effectively in one situation can in a new operation be the wrong steps that stifle an operation even before it has come to life. A new agency must fit itself into a pattern and watch the opportunities made available to it to move forward and make "Brownie points."

A list of important people in county government when made up included such diverse elements as the county executive, his secretary, the deputy county executive, the public relations officer, the county attorney, the secretary to the Board of Supervisors, the supervisors themselves, the attorney assigned to handle county contracts, the purchasing agent, the comptroller, the budget officer, the director of Bureau of Management Information, the head of Record Services, the head of the Office

Harold L. Roth

of Building Services, the head of the Department of Public Works, the superintendent of recreation and parks, the hospital administrator. This is not a complete list, but one that gives an idea of diversification in a government agency. Your own list will be based on sources of cooperation and your judgment of the government operations, but you can never tell in advance what kind of services come out of what department. The trick is not to cut off connections before finding out. A new director must be patient until the lines of communications are developed.

Government has rules, but it is in the observance or non-observance of these rules that ground can be gained, structure developed, plans moved forward or set back. A new agency has a honeymoon period even if the policy is that the county executive makes his own way. The bliss of not knowing enables one to ask questions. By asking questions properly, one moves ahead. By reacting properly to answers one moves further ahead.

Movement ahead is sometimes something so trivial as telling the county executive's secretary where to get a certain travel magazine. The contact rendered through as simple a service as that facilitates easy access to the county executive's office and smooths the way for contact with other executives there. Suddenly the library is put on the routing list for releases from that office, receives minutes of the Board of Supervisors, and is invited to special county functions. The best part is a tacit agreement that requests to the county executive's office will not be conveniently lost, but will be passed for effective actions.

When a starting budget is small, there is no alternative but to attempt to develop out of the budgets of others, or on available materials. The slogan in this government operation, as passed along, was "If you've got a desk and a chair, you're in business." The agency is fortunate enough to have a secretary and a telephone. In local parlance the agency is told, "You are two years ahead on starting time." One takes advantage of opportunities when possible, and builds on them. One also learns the language of the territory while learning the territory.

This agency's move ahead resulted from having been based on a service complex which was developing another institution.

As the new institution developed, the administration moved to concentrate on its growth by divesting itself temporarily of activities unrelated to the reference library. Temporary moves sometimes become reasonably permanent. Support for the library agency grew even though the supervisor activities were reduced.

The political forces noted earlier were gathering themselves for an action to change the political leadership for the next three years. Earlier on, an action project to gain immediate political support for the library and to present the image of a producing agency had been presented to the county administration. It was recommended that this be pushed for implementation to both sides of the political aisle. The building project was again suggested as an action program. The director and his board calculated and agreed to stay away from the second proposal. The fear was that the building would be supported or not supported strictly as a political action without concern for the service benefits to be derived, but rather as a physical structure, the image of someone's contribution to the county.

A final proposal was made that the board members and the library administration present on a face–to–face basis the story of the library to each of the members of the Board of Supervisors (the legislators of the county), so they would be aware of what had been done to date and the rationale of the total proposed project. Both political parties were visited. The results, although not assessable at that time, lead to the belief that all legislators favor the library. During the election campaign itself, the library was not an issue.

The library continued to direct its activities to professional matters. Administrators of each library group were visited. The director reviewed old acquaintances. Each institution of higher education has been visited, fifty percent of the public libraries have been visited, and almost all professional meetings have been attended.

The library story in terms of its philosophy has been told to all members of the public library systems, to trustees of the libraries, to the directors of the academic libraries, to certain department heads in the government, to planning officials on a bi-

Harold L. Roth

county and county basis, to some service clubs, and to individuals as well as to the Division of Library Development.

In each case the story included activity anticipated for the next year, with a statement of the budget being requested for operating purposes, for capital purposes, and for the special project. The director, with the support of this board, pushed for a sum ten times the original operating budget. The request was presented to the budget offices and the rest of the time was spent waiting for the political dust to settle.

With the election results in, a complete change in government took place. The library's position was uncertain, but the base agency, in which its planning forces were housed, looked as though it might be changed completely. With this in mind, the library administration continued its direction of philosophical growth and support of the mind. Political appointments were made to replace appointees of the previous administration. The library remained untouched except that the budget was cut, like all others, and its funds were twice rather than ten times its original budget.

A new base agency administrator was appointed whose responsibilities are still being developed. The board president and director visited him and a rapport has developed to the extent that the library will have a complete operating base of its own, clerical staff five times what it had at the beginning, and professional staff four times as large. The excellent relations with the new government strengthens the support of plans for the new library in the county executive's "State of the County" report. Money is not everything, but support is.

The relationship of a chartered public library, albeit one with academic responsibilities, to academic libraries is frequently somewhat tenuous. Cooperation in this case has been furthered by budget tightening, economic stress, and the offer of cooperation. A developing consortium among the academic institutions has made it possible for the reference library to offer cooperation and thereby to develop a strong base. By expressing a willingness to work with college and university libraries and to plan in depth nonduplicative functions, the reference library will move forward.

Three members of the reference library board represent three major colleges and universities. Each one spoke to his administration and offered the library's services in the cooperative effort. The economic tightness of the times made it possible to gain acceptance on the first offer. This, then, becomes another avenue of public support.

The business community has been approached through its agency for business information, the local Chamber of Commerce. This agency is hoping for greater depth than its own resources can supply. If it sees action, the agency promises support from the business community.

The Nassau County Reference Library has moved since March 1970, when it had only a Board of Trustees, a library director, a secretary, a small amount of money for incidentals, a room, a desk, chair, and some telephone service, to its present stage in which it has the use of almost an entire building, four librarians, six clerks, a budget at least twice as large as its predecessor, and effective support from the county administration. It has developed a newsletter and an explanatory leaflet on the library. Its next project is to provide plans for a functioning library. The next hope is that funding will make it possible to move ahead with construction, collection, building, staff development, and service.

Harold L. Roth

Index

Carson, Rachel, 13
Cassettes, use of in children's rooms, 126
Castagna, Edwin, 58
Celebration weeks, in academic library, 138–139
Censorship, community and, 77–78
Chamber of Commerce, small public library and, 85
Charles Scribner's Sons, 93
Chartered public library, vs. academic library, 229
Chicago, University of, 133
Chicago Public Library, 133
Children, involvement of in library work, 127–128
Children's Animal Fair, 91
Children's art exhibits, 89, 124
Children's Book Week, small public library, 79–80
Children's librarian
  adult groups and, 122–123
  in-service training by, 122
  obligation of to meet people, 120–122
  service by, 121–122
  specialized agencies and, 122–123
Children's room, 117–131
  cassettes in, 126
  Chamber of Commerce calendar and, 130
  children's cooperation and participation in, 127
  collections in, 125–126

courtesy and friendliness in, 120–121
junior volunteers for, 124
lecture-demonstrations in, 126
library-sponsored programs in, 126
news releases from, 129
non-library story hours in, 128–129
outside trips and, 128
phonograph records and, 125–126
pre-school programs of, 130
publicity for, 129–130
"public relations" concept in, 131
roundtable discussion group in, 125
service organizations and, 130
story-oriented programs and, 126
Teen Program Committee in, 127
Christmas parties, small public library, 89–90
Churchill, Winston S., 92
Civil War Centennial, 138
Cobbett, William, 138
College library, *see* Academic library
College student, library and, 135
Colorado, University of, 151
Columbia University, 179, 195
Committee on Public Information, 6

children's librarian and, 123
educational institutions and,
206
school library and, 106,
110–111
Participatory democracy,
concept of, 145
Pegboard displays, 141
Pennsylvania State Library, 27
Performance, concept of, 148
Phonograph records, in child-
ren's rooms, 125–126
Photographs, proper use of, 24
Photo library, *New York
Times,* 171
Pied Piper Story Hour, 79, 91
Planning, cooperative, 206
Playboy, 86
Posters, 32–33, 36, 44
in academic library, 141
artwork for, 37
children's room and, 129
*Practical Administration of
Public Libraries,* 221
Pratt Institute, 165, 179
Prizes and drawings, 57
PTA, *see* Parent Teachers
Association
"Public," defined, 105
Public Affairs Council Bul-
letin (YWCA), 129
Publications
artwork in, 35–36
of library, 30–32
"Public-be-damned" period
(1865–1900), 5
Public information, era of
(1900–1914), 5

Public information desk, in
metropolitan library, 38
Publicity
for children's room, 129
faith in, 5
see also News release; Public relations
Public library
children's room in, *see*
Children's room
research collection in, 18
vs. school library, 103, 108–
111
small, *see* Small public
library
see also Metropolitan
library
Public library of Cincinnati, 43
Public Library System, Long
Island, 209
Public opinion, power of, 6
Public relations
for academic libraries, 133–
149
as art, 46
as art of meeting people
well, 120
in children's room, 117–131
in cooperative suburban library system, 49–67
defined, vii, 3, 103–104
external, 20
good performance as, 148
good service in, 18–21, 119
good vs. bad, 71
immediacy of, 38
internal, 41–42, 147
knowledge of public in, 46

children's room and, 127
Television
    presentation script for, 27
    as publicity medium, 26,
        28, 79, 173
    school budget presentation
        in, 210
    school library and, 99
    and small public library, 85
    spot announcements on,
        26–28
Textbooks, school library
    and, 100
"Thank you" letters, 82
Theodore Roosevelt Centen-
    nial, 138
"3 Rs + 2" program, 208–210
Tolstoi, Leo, 138
Toulouse-Lautrec, Henri, 138
Trustees
    for developing library, 224–
        225
    in small public library, 73
    workshops for, 62–63

United Federation of Teach-
    ers, 111
United Nations Week, 138
United States Office of Edu-
    cation, 155
United States Steel Corp., 6
Unserved patrons, public rela-
    tions help to, 60–62

Vail, Theodore N., 6

Walck, Henry Z., 93
Wallace, Sarah Leslie, 52
Walla Walla (Wash.) Public
    Library, 93
Wall Street Journal, 86
Welcome Wagon, small pub-
    lic library and, 87–88
Westbury (N.Y.) *Times,* 49
Westbury Memorial Library,
    49
Western Reserve University,
    179
Wheeler, Joseph L., 221
Whyte, William H., Jr., 185
Willard, Daniel, 6
Williams, Barbara Chapman,
    74
Williamson, Merritt A., 183,
    190
Wilson, Woodrow, 6
Women's Church Clinic, Cairo
    (Ga.), 83
Women's Golfing Association,
    small public library and,
Women's groups, cooperation
    with, 83
Workshops
    in Nassau County Library
        System, 59–60
    in regional system, 45
    for trustees, 62–63

Yakima Valley (Wash.), Re-
    gional Library, 93
YWCA, 129

Ziebold, Edna, 100